HEATHER A.R. ASALS is a member of the Department of English at York University, Toronto.

Equivocation replaced Thomistic analogy as a means of predicating God in the minds of many seventeenth-century divines. In this study, Professor Asals analyses George Herbert's use of language as a method of devotion in his major cycle poem, *The Temple*. Tracing the logical notion of equivocation (here the extensive use of puns and pun-like verbal devices) as predication through other influences on his poetry, she argues that the very basis of Herbert's work lies in its responsibility in predicating God as One and Love.

Asals explains that, for Herbert, the act of writing a poem – the actual handwriting – was a sacramental and ceremonial act of worship recreating Christ's death on the cross: ink becomes blood. The sign on the printed page points sacramentally to the blood it signifies. Thus, the domain of Herbert's poetry reaches from earth to heaven and from heaven to earth.

Continuing with an examination of Herbert's language, including aspects of phonology, morphology, and syntax, Asals reveals its two-fold significance in expression and meaning. Through a detailed reading of the entire corpus, she investigates the profound influence of Augustinianism and Wisdom literature on the way poetry works and explores the meaning of gesture and its importance to Herbert's Anglicanism – his belief in the importance of ceremony.

In the final chapter, on the *topos* of Magdalene, its relationship to Herbert's mother, and his mother's importance to his writing, Asals argues that Anglicanism as a way to God (and God as a way to himself) is at the very core of Herbert's poetics.

This book establishes a new critical milieu in which Herbert may be interpreted and sheds new light on the poetry of other writers of the period.

HEATHER A.R. ASALS

Equivocal Predication

George Herbert's Way to God

UNIVERSITY OF TORONTO PRESS
Toronto Buffalo London

© University of Toronto Press 1981
Toronto Buffalo London
Printed in Canada
ISBN 0-8020-5536-2

Canadian Cataloguing in Publication Data

Asals, Heather A.R. (Heather Anne Ross), 1940–
  Equivocal predication
  Bibliography: p.
  Includes index.
  ISBN 0-8020-5536-2
  1. Herbert, George, 1593–1633 — Criticism and
  interpretation. 2. Herbert, George, 1593–1633 —
  Religion and ethics. 3. Christianity in literature.
  I. Title.
  PR3508.A82   821'.3   C81-094129-5

This book is published with the assistance of a grant from the Andrew W. Mellon
Foundation to the University of Toronto Press.

2186862

In memory of Elizabeth Anne
and Benjamin Stuart

*ἄφετε τὰ παιδία ἔρχεσθαι πρός με καὶ μὴ κωλύετε αὐτά τῶν γὰρ τοιούτων
ἐστὶν ἡ βασιλεία τοῦ θεοῦ.*

Acknowledgments

It has taken me years of reading Herbert to discover what is 'hid' with Christ beneath the deceptively polished surface of his poetry. And through those years and the months spent in the Folger, the Cambridge, and the British libraries I have come to owe many practical and spiritual debts, and I wish to express my gratitude here. The Canada Council twice, once by a Research Grant and again by a Leave Grant, enabled me to do the reading in Renaissance texts which has led to many of the discoveries in this book. My work on Herbert began under the direction of Barbara Lewalski who has remained a friend and special advisor in the years following. Amy Charles, Albert Labriola, John Shawcross, and Paul Stanwood have also read the manuscript and provided both useful and encouraging reactions. Janet Patterson acted as a 'trial student' reader, made some very helpful suggestions about presentation, and helped me in the preparation of the bibliography. Chris Marks was instrumental in preparing the index. Geri Dasgupta, Kim Echlin, and Ian Sowtan are to be thanked for aiding me with my proofreading. Prudence Tracy of the University of Toronto Press deserves a tribute for her friendly and brilliant handling of the manuscript. And Judy Williams of the Press did a superb job of copy-editing.

I regret that neither my father nor my mother lived to see the publication of this book. I remember here especially my father, Francis Graham Ross, who saw to my education and my early acquaintance with the classics. But more than any other single human being, my husband, Rick, merits my special thanks for years of holding my hand 'while I did write': he helped by his companionship through the otherwise lonely journey of writing a book and by his continually insightful literary and theological conversation in our married life. The dedication of this book expresses the deep sorrow which we both share and our faith that the vision of George Herbert is not ungrounded.

Contents

Preface

It is my earnest desire that no future student of George Herbert will stumble across this technical study of the dynamics of Herbert's religious language without having first read the basic book on Herbert by Joseph Summers. In many ways I consider this to be a sequel to that book: a more advanced reading of Herbert's religion and art. What concerns me most here is the art of predication: how Herbert makes claims to what *is*. Herbert found, I believe, a method of predication which transcends the usual grammatical subject-predicate format; and his poetry became the non-prosaic predication of that 'is' which is in the *being* of God, existing beyond time and the time-bound form of sentence structure.

The material is difficult, for it asks us to relinquish some of our everyday assumptions. I expect two things of my reader: 1 / that he have open a copy of the complete poetry of Herbert as he reads, for I move from poem to poem (Herbert criticism has, I believe, been crippled by an effort to analyse at length single poems out of the context of the whole); 2 / that he accept, for the time being anyway, Herbert's brand of Christianity as his own – it is in this way that any reader will best understand him. The audience I expect to reach includes theologians and linguists as well as literary critics because I think Herbert should be of equal interest to them as to us who are used to teaching him.

The introduction requires careful attention, for it is there that we first encounter the basic difficulty of the language of Herbert's poetry: it defies arithmetic and says that *one thing equals two*, or, 'A sonne is light and fruit.' In order to understand precisely what is meant by the observation of several critics that Herbert's poetry is 'sacramental,' one must begin with the observation that the statement of the Consecration, '*This is my Body*,' is one of predication. And one must realize, in addition, that the sacramental predication is fundamentally, in Anglican theology anyway, a claim that 'This' (one thing) is *both* 'bread' *and* 'my Body' (two things).

For some time we have been aware of the fact that seventeenth-century poetry tends to pun. Now I think we may have found a good reason why, when we anatomize the method whereby Herbert makes two things equal one in the surface-tension of language itself. This phenomenon of the two-in-one of language is, I argue, the verbal sign and evidence that George Herbert is a priest in *The Temple*, in his poetry itself. I think that in what follows we find a literary vocabulary for dealing with what otherwise remains a biographical fact. The destiny of Herbert's sacred poetry, as I understand it, is not only to 'appear' or 'seem' temporarily to the human heart, but ultimately to touch that which *is and ever shall be* in God, to erect a bridge from the fading multiplicity of the world of time to the infinite *oneness* which is in God.

EQUIVOCAL PREDICATION

Introduction

Holy Equivocation

What comes to mind more than anything else as I reflect at this point of departure is that what I have to say has all been said before, that 'The thing that hath been, it is that which shall be; and that which is done is that which shall be done; and there is no new thing under the sun' (Ecclesiastes 1:9). Once, in conversation with Margaret Bottrall in Cambridge, I came to feel this acutely: that there is no *new thing* here and that my function here is to make whole, to integrate some of the present disparities in Herbert criticism. It is not my own particular mode or idiom to begin a critical book on Herbert by demonstrating the limitations of what has been said to date about Herbert: anyone who writes about Herbert has courage of a very important kind and a commitment to the man and his work which must, by necessity, transcend the ordinary. From personal experience I think it is fair to say that the scholar of Herbert's poetry undergoes once again, or recognizes, Herbert's many spiritual-literary combats. It is not lightly that I point to Herbert's complaint in 'Gratefulnesse' as the original version of my own: 'But thou didst reckon, when at first / Thy word our hearts and hands did crave, / What it would come to at the worst' – 'Perpetuall knockings at thy doore.'[1]

Because the 'wit' of the metaphysical poets is too frequently blamed on the reader-critic as outlandish invention, I begin by outlining here the major places where I share in the recognitions of others. Most obviously, the hermeneutic criticism of Stanley Fish and Barbara Lewalski is an area which it is difficult for a Herbert critic now to avoid confronting: Herbert himself is very preoccupied with hermeneutics, as he reveals not only in his statements about 'Catechizing' but also in his illuminating comments about 'Arguing,' 'Knowledge,' and 'Divinity,' to name just a few more hermeneutic sections in

The Country Parson. In her essay entitled 'Typology and Poetry' Barbara
Lewalski argues the case for the importance of the 'Protestant emphasis' in the
poetry of Herbert, Vaughan, and Marvell, on the 'individual Christian as an
antitype of the Old Testament types,' and she locates the destiny of the entire
typological relationship in the 'heart of the speaker' of a poem.[2] Taking his
cue from Lewalski's Protestant emphasis in interpreting Herbert, Stanley
Fish also de-emphasizes the finality of history and icons (ontology, perma-
nent significance, and outward forms) in favour of the inner workings of the
heart as Herbert's own hermeneutical preference: 'An ambiguous text is
ambiguously interpreted,' he suggests, 'hermeneutics merely reproducing the
conditions that call it into being. Wherever one looks into these texts one
finds instability, *not of the simple and comforting kind that offers itself as an
ontology,* but of the kind that operates to prevent interpretive rest.'[3] Even the
Editor, as Max Patrick suggests at the end of his 'Editor as Critic' paper on
Herbert, becomes necessarily involved in the process known as 'hermeneutics.' Herbert, Patrick observes, by 'creating structural correspondences to his
themes in individual poems and by fusing thought, structure, and pattern into
an organic whole ... equates the thoughts with the patterns.'[4]

Herbert spells out his own Biblical hermeneutics most precisely in 'The H.
Scriptures (II)': 'This verse marks that, and both do make a motion / Unto a
third, that ten leaves off doth lie: / ... Such are thy secrets, which my life
makes good, / And comments on thee: for in ev'ry thing / Thy words do finde
me out, & parallels bring.' The aptness of hermeneutic criticism to *The
Temple* is underscored by the reflexive quality of the poetry of *The Temple*:
its many comments about what poetry is and should be, and how we are to
understand, constitute one of its most notable features. So, 'hermeneutics' in
Herbert is a topic which I consider to be very important and one which cannot
be overlooked. What bothers me is the growing tendency to turn *The Temple*
into a 'Protestant' poem, a tendency which neglects Herbert's own personal
commitment to Anglicanism and the story told in Walton of Herbert turning
to Edmund Duncon on his deathbed: ' "I desire you to pray with me," '
Walton quotes Herbert as requesting, continuing, 'Mr. Duncon asked him,
"What prayers?" to which Mr. Herbert's answer was, "O sir, the prayers of
my mother the Church of England; no other prayers are equal to them." '[5]

In April 1977, I was sitting in the British Library reading one of the last
sermons of William Laud and I was 'struck,' as by one of Herbert's 'starres'
('Artillerie'), that we who are writing about the literature of the seventeenth
century should learn to appreciate all that we can of those differences in
attitude toward prayer, ceremony, gesture and vestment, and the Eucharist,
which shook the ship of Church-State in seventeenth-century England, mat-

ters so grave to them who lived then that a man such as Laud was willing to lay down his life for them. What bothers me about Fish's reading of Herbert in his *The Living Temple* (a book which I, otherwise, admire greatly) is his dismissal of ontology and, with it, Herbert's own attachment to the principles of the *via media* which argued the necessity of outward form and assumed the validity of a ceremonious ontology. I disagree wholeheartedly with Patrick Grant's assertion that Herbert is 'a more assuredly Protestant theologian than Donne,'[6] and my purpose here is partly to restore Herbert as a specifically Anglican poet. In 1954 Margaret Bottrall spoke well for this position: Herbert, she says, found the *via media* of the Anglican Church 'exactly to his liking' – 'Herbert himself clearly had a fondness for the ancient observances of the church.'[7] George Herbert, Festugière remarks in 1971, 'de même que son ami Nicholas Ferrar à Little Gidding, est essentiellement fidèle à la Church of England.'[8] Most recently, in her fine biography of Herbert, Amy Charles brings into focus a large number of biographical details (especially the Andrewes-Herbert connection) which suggest that it is not out of line to 'reclaim' Herbert as an Anglican, and even, what we now call a 'high' Anglican.[9] As I argue in my last chapter, the figure of the Mother-Church (both Church and Mother, Magdalene Herbert) is at the centre of Herbert's metaphorical system (and the system of language itself). As Herbert is keen on reminding us in his Latin poetry, it was his Mother who *taught him how to write*.

At the core of the question about how one should interpret Herbert (and how he would have himself interpreted as he subjects his own poetry to interpretation) is the Eucharistic dispute among Herbert's readers: can a poem contain Christ? As I see it there are two Herbert-on-the-Eucharist camps (fewer than the camps which take sides on the Eucharist itself): those who believe that we cannot discuss the idea of the Real Presence in Herbert's theology or his poetry, and those who believe that the Real Presence is central to Herbert's theological poetry and is, even, its essence. The polarity is obvious. Sister Thekla argues on the one hand that Herbert 'does not assign to the Eucharist the independent reality of Presence,'[10] and Richard Hughes argues on the other hand in his reading of Herbert's conclusive 'Love (III)' that the last three lines of the poem 're-unite the temporal and spiritual, even as the doctrine of the Real Presence in the Eucharist re-unites the two.'[11] Most readers of Herbert sense the poetic-artistic importance of settling the dogmatic issue of Herbert's attitude toward the Sacrament, and I, for one, concur absolutely with Richard Hughes when he says that 'What Herbert felt about the Incarnation is, without question, the central issue of his poetry' – 'he saw poetry itself as a miniature version of the Incarnation.[12] More precisely, I think that C.A. Patrides hits the mark in the very suggestive introduction to his edition of Herbert when he claims that the Eucharist is 'the marrow of Herbert's sensibility.'[13] As M.M. Mahood observes in her *Poetry and Humanism*, the importance of the Eucharist to poetry is that in the Sacrament the two planes of life, earthly and heavenly, intersect.[14] Louis Martz has made a case for *The Temple* as 'mental' and 'spiritual' communion,[15] but my own concern with the evidence of the celebration of that Feast in the poetry of *The Temple* is primarily verbal. The eucharistic sacrifice in *The Temple*, I argue, is the sacrifice of language itself: the poetry is eucharistic because it consecrates the 'creature' of language as the ontological bridge to the divine.

It will become clear in the course of my discussion of the Sacrament and its relation to Herbert's theory of language in *The Temple* that I disagree with the working premises and the conclusions of Malcolm Ross in his *Poetry and Dogma*. An eloquent book which registers distress (in which I share) at the 'spectacle of analogical symbol dissolving into simple metaphor,'[16] Ross's *Poetry and Dogma* employs what I consider to be questionable materials of modern theological commentary and, consequently, comes to what I feel to be some wrong conclusions, most notably that the Reformers destroy the symbolic reach of the Eucharist and, hence, a symbol's ontological claim. While recognizing rightly that it is in Anglican poetry, 'hovering precariously as it must between Catholic and Protestant symbol, that one is able to sense most vividly the poignant dilemma of the Christian artist,'[17] Ross is wrong, I believe, in his assumption that analogy alone can create ontological relevance: this is not what Herbert's contemporaries, or Herbert, assumed. And Ross himself wants to create a loophole for Herbert in his scheme by making a case for his mysticism (otherworldliness) on the one hand and his 'Catholic carnality' on the other.[18] I find myself repeatedly returning to the rightness of the work of Rosemond Tuve in 1952 in her reading of 'The Sacrifice' and her notion that Herbert's 'symbolic imagery is precisely similar to the liturgical way of using it,' by ironic contrast, dramatizing man's 'blind misreading of the real ... that gap between what truth is, and how man perceives it.'[19] To suggest that man misreads the real is to suggest the imperfection of his hermeneutic capacities. But it is not to suggest that the Real is not Present. To dramatize man as misreader is to dramatize irony, paradox, and tension as the nature of the Eucharist and the materials of language in 'The Church.' My largest goal here is to offer a vocabulary for discussing seventeenth-century poetry as Eucharistic (when it is) and Herbert's language as transcendent. Herbert's language is 'a language which can convey more than words can enclose in their definable meanings,' Tuve comments at the end of her *Reading* of George Herbert.[20] Patrides, too, speaks of 'the way language and even individual words look beyond themselves.'[21] The *key* to Herbert's use of language, I suggest, rests not in the absence of analogy but in the presence of equivocacy.

My working title for this book was for some time 'The Language of Canaan,' for that phrase expresses the directive of Herbert's language. William Perkins, for one, defines such language as that 'whereby a man endued with the spirit of adoption, unfainedly calleth upon the name of God in Christ, and so consequently doth as it were, familiarly talke and speake with God ... For man must first be able to talke with God, before hee can be able wisely to talke with man.'[22] And John Boys, while explaining the need for the 'new song,' describes its singer as one who speaks the language of Canaan: 'hee speaketh with a new tongue, and walkes in ỹ new wayes: and therefore doth new things, and sings new songs: his language is not of *Babylon*, or *Egypt*, but of *Canaan*: his communication doth edify men, his song glorifie God.'[23] Both Perkins and Boys are, of course, Puritans and therefore tend to stress the inwardness of religious language. Herbert's language is *both* of Egypt and of Canaan: it attempts to make what is manifestly here and on earth (the outward hieroglyph of the poem itself) *relate to* heaven and the beyond. For Herbert, language is spoken on the way, it is the way, to the Promised Land; it builds a ladder to heaven and creates an ontological bridge to the Being of God. Herbert understood himself to be at work in a language which aspired for transcendency, a language which *racked* him between the great 'distances,' the 'extent' of heaven and earth.

Herbert's poetry repeatedly asks us to examine his poetic language: the 'I like our language' of 'The Sonne,' the 'Is it no verse' of 'Jordan (I),' the 'Brave language' of 'Frailitie,' and the 'Lovely enchanting language' of 'The Forerunners' are all signposts leading us to the observation that Herbert's poetry continually subjects itself to ontological scrutiny and asks, 'What manner of thing *am* I?' Once again, I am not the first to suggest that the subject of language in Herbert's poetry is an important topic. Joseph Summers devotes a chapter of his book on Herbert, 'The Proper Language,' to Herbert's linguistic ideals, and Summers there reaches conclusions that must still today, twenty-five years later, remain the point of departure for any Herbert student. The chief consideration, he argues, 'was not how to convey personal experience honestly but how to use language most effectively for the subject, the aim, and the intended audience of specific compositions.'[24] Herbert's 'wit,' Summers maintains, 'is evidence that language, like man, has constantly to be renewed in order to stay alive.'[25] Arnold Stein discusses not 'wit' but 'plainness' in Herbert and, although I find his remarks about the importance of 'brevity,' for instance, most germane, I find it hard to accept his concept of Herbert's plainness as 'an art by which he may tell the truth to himself and God.'[26] Although Coburn Freer offers an interesting observation about Herbert's language when he mentions the discrepancy in Herbert's poetry between the way a poem behaves and the way Herbert says it behaves, I find a statement such as 'One way of rejecting earthly joys is to write an ugly poem'[27] totally inadmissible. Mark Taylor's notion of Herbert's Augustinianism providing 'a model of his own spiritual ascendency' is much closer to the truth. But I do not agree with him that 'Herbert is always aware that words are only signs,' and I object to the notion that 'Herbert was consciously anti-metaphysical in his views of poetic style and was a devotee of Puritan plainness.'[28]

In certain ways it would be fair to say that what I formulate here is but an extension of Stanley Fish's germinal 1972 essay on Herbert in *Self-Consuming Artifacts*. I am totally convinced of the validity of the following insights, which Fish captures in that essay: that in Herbert's poetry 'words tend to lose their referential fixity,'[29] that 'To stop saying amiss is not only to stop distinguishing "this" from "that," but to stop distinguishing oneself from God,'[30] and that 'Herbert avoids saying amiss in the context of a perspective he would have us transcend.'[31] As I continue, I will speak more directly to the question he raises there, 'If insight into God's omnipresence is violated by the very act of predication ("this or that is"), how does a poet who is committed to that insight practise his craft?' But I should also mention that I am very impressed indeed by a few incidental remarks made by Helen Vendler in a book about which I, generally speaking, have grave reservations. She speaks very much in tune with what I consider to be the central chord of Herbert's poetry when she discusses Herbert's 'pruning' of language in 'Paradise' ('Each pruning, as Herbert's hieroglyph shows, engenders a new word'),[32] and she very rightly considers the 'false etymologies' in Herbert's Echo poem ('Heaven') to be central to his poetic method – 'We should like to think that such natural opposites and obverses and parallels had a "natural" linguistic relation' (they *should* have, she concludes).[33]

As I see it, what has been best said about Herbert's idea of language to date is very much in line with what has been remarked on as his concern with the Many and the One. In 1936 Helen White spoke quite precisely of Herbert's poetic imagination: 'However it may lift its head towards the One, its roots are in the Many'[34] – 'a reintegrated world of order came home to their destinies in the One Love.'[35] In an interesting reading of 'Providence,' Virginia Mollenkott pursues that theme by claiming that the central motif of 'Providence' is 'that of the One in the Many and the Many in the One.'[36] Surely it would not be premature to deduce at this point that Herbert's philosophical-theological concern with the relation of the Many to the One is an interest which includes his poetic practice of punning (the many and the one of language itself). Mary Ellen Rickey does some superb work with Herbert's punning in the 'Sacred Quibbles' chapter of her *Utmost Art*. She says that the pun for Herbert points up the discrepancy between what is and what should be.[37] My reservation about her work there is just that she does not carry things far enough: she suggests that the point of Herbert's punning is 'to sound his imagerial notes in polyphonic fashion.'[38] Eventually (in chapter two), I will define the ontological function of the pun, understood logically as 'equivocation.' Punning (or equivocation), the Many and the One linguistically expressed, is, certainly, the centre of the *tension* in Herbert's poetic language. The 'secret wit' of Herbert's poetry, Judith Dundas comments, is the 'recognition that religion is nothing without paradox.'[39] As we turn to the rules of logic by which Herbert learned his ontological 'spelling,' we must realize at once the lucidity and the profundity of M.M. Mahood's comment about Herbert's love of homophones: 'what Herbert particularly liked about the English language is our homophones.'[40] Punning, then, is not just a phenomenon but a principle in Herbert's poetry: it expresses his vision of the universe, as does his use of the hyphen ('Bitter-sweet'), a device which I myself have adopted for the explication of the two-in-one of Herbert's poetry.

II   A LOGICAL VOCABULARY

In the passage that has become to logicians, philosophers, and theologians the *locus classicus* of methods of predication, Aristotle at the very beginning of his *Categories* makes a statement which structures and directs almost all discussion of meaning and language from the thirteenth through the seventeenth centuries. 'Things are *equivocally* named,' the passage begins, 'when they have the *name only* in common, the definition (or statement of essence) corresponding with the name being different.'[41] 'Equivocation' (the term of a logician), 'pun' (the more likely term of a modern critic), and 'homonym' (a more exact translation of Aristotle's Greek: ὁμώνυμα), all amount to the same thing: one *word* equals two *definitions*. Herbert spells out the rules of equivocation in 'The Sonne': 'sonne' is both 'light and fruit,' and so 'in *one word* our Lords humilitie / We turn upon him in *a sense most true*.' This is what I consider to be Herbert's formal 'apology' for equivocation; homonymous language turns to a 'sense most true.' Herbert explains and justifies the texture of his language, his poetry, and his Church ('The Church') in 'The Sonne': it is made of the stuff of apologetics. This is the heart of the matter, and all that follows builds upon this evidence that Herbert himself seems to have spelt out the rules for reading his poetry equivocally.

'Things are *univocally* named,' Aristotle continues in the same passage from the *Categories*, when 'the name means the same in each case – has the same definition corresponding.' In univocal predication *two words* equal *one definition*: its procedure is the opposite of equivocal predication (where *one word* equals *two definitions*). Whereas equivocation is basically 'homonym' (or 'pun' – 'sonne'), univocation is rather 'synonym' (συνώνυμα), and it is capable of operating as 'paradox' when two antonymous words are equated as meaning one thing. Univocal predication is more characteristic of the poetry of Donne than of Herbert: 'Death and conception' (two words) 'in mankinde is one' (one meaning), Donne argues. But univocation can be found in Herbert's 'Providence' (most prominently), operating not paradoxically but 'privatively' (as logicians call it): 'Light without winde is glasse: warm without weight / Is wooll and furre: cool without closeness, shade: / Speed without pains, a horse: tall without height, / A servile hawk: low without losse, a spade.' 'Each thing that is,' Herbert explains (making the case for equivocacy at the end of 'Providence'), 'although in *use and name* / It go for *one*, hath *many wayes* in store / To honour thee.' Herbert tells us twice that we must read 'Providence' differently from the rest of his poetry: 'and so each hymne thy fame / Extolleth many wayes, *yet this one more*,' and 'and so I give thee praise / In all my other hymns, *but in this twice*.' The uniqueness of 'Providence' rests in its heroic attempt to relate oneness-in-language (equivocacy) to oneness-in-things (univocacy) and to offer this as the total *Oneness* of God: 'Thou art in all things one,' by the logic of equivocacy, 'and in each thing many,' by the logic of univocacy, 'For thou art infinite' (not 'definite') 'in one and all.'

One might very well ask at this point, 'What is to be gained by changing terminology, by trading in the usual terms of the literary critic (pun, paradox) for the less familiar terms of the logician (equivocation, univocation), by exchanging the "open hand" for the "closed fist"?' We must, simply because it is in logical terms that the function of religious language is understood by the English Renaissance. It is also in logical terms that the Sacrament is discussed and explained apologetically in the English Renaissance. And, finally, it is in a logical context that we must place Herbert's ontological 'spelling,' his predication of what 'is' in the 'I AM' of God (which is his *name*). Herbert learns the art of spelling in the Being of God through equivocation and univocation which lead him to the 'one and all' of God: 'After so many deaths I *live and write*; / ... And relish versing.' The poet is 'the worlds high Priest' in his role as equivocator-univocator, and it is incumbent on him to re-integrate the one and the all with the materials of language. Language itself is the *sacrifice* in *The Temple*, and the poet's role is sacred in that 'he doth present / The sacrifice for all.' Herbert *breaks the host of language itself*; he *breaks* the Word itself. And it is such breaking of the letter of the word which releases it from terrestrial Egypt and permits it to ascend-transcend to celestial Canaan.

Of course, it is Aristotle's third term, 'analogy,' or 'paranym' (παρώνυμα), which becomes the basis of much of St Thomas's metaphysic, his own ontological re-integration of the universe, joining being with Being, love with Love, light with Light. Analogy, considered by Thomas and a multitude of others who followed him to be the 'middle term' between equivocacy and univocacy, creates a bridge between entity and essence, between word and definition. But it is a bridge which George Herbert and seventeenth-century Anglican theology as a rule could not accept. In a remark she chooses not to pursue, Rosemond Tuve says very rightly that Herbert is not a Thomist and that, for instance, he stubbornly resists attempts to see human love as analogous to divine love, 'abstaining from phrases which would claim reciprocity in the love between God and man.'[42] But in spite of Herbert's rejection of Thomas's metaphysic, his poetry is heavily under the influence of Aristotle's *Categories* (it is extremely logical): Herbert predicates, differentiates, and spins lines, stanzas, and even poems out of the Aristotelian 'predicaments' of 'what' (substance), 'how large' (quantity), 'what sort of thing' (quality), 'related to what' (relation), 'where' (place), 'when' (time), 'what attitude' (posture, position), 'how circumstanced' (condition), 'what doing' (action), 'how passive and what suffering' (affection). In 'Discipline,' for instance, Herbert categorizes 'Love' according to Aristotle's predicaments: 'Love is swift of foot,' he writes of its *condition*, continuing, 'Love's a man of warre, / And can shoot, / And hit from farre.'

In a crucial passage in his *A Body of Divinitie*, James Ussher puts forth a reaction, characteristic of seventeenth-century England, to the question, 'Why can there be no perfect definition of God given?' Every definition, he answers, 'is an explication of the nature of a thing defined by words expressing the materiall and formall cause thereof, but of the first cause there can be no causes, therefore no words to express them.'[43] Ussher does little here to offer an alternative to the courageous efforts of Thomas to predicate God, but he adds something which is a clue to and an important indication of the philosophical system which lies behind the equivocacy of metaphysical poetry:

for these over-reaching termes of thing, beeing, somewhat, nature, &c. which seem to contain the Word of God as well as all other things created by him, doe not expresse any materiall cause of God, neither doe they contain these words God and creature, as the generall doth his specials or kinds *but are spoken of them equivocally, so that the tearm onely, and not the definition of the tearm doth agree to them.*[44]

Some of the properties (or attributes) of God can be seen as 'weak shadows and glimpses' in the creatures (wisdom, holiness, justice, mercy, etc.), Ussher continues, but *those that are peculiar to the divine Essence* (simpleness, infiniteness, eternity) cannot be found as 'substance' or 'accident.'[45] Fourteen years later (1658) in his *Certain Disputations of Right to Sacraments and the True Nature of Visible Christianity*, Richard Baxter argues the case for the propriety of equivocacy even more cogently. In the 'Logicks commonly read in the Schools,' Baxter testifies, *'Omne Analogum est AEquivocum'*: *'Scotus* maintaineth, that *inter Univoca & Aequivoca non datur medium'* (1. Dist. 8. q. 2).[46] There is no 'middle term.' In the 'highest matters about the Attributes and Works of God,' he explains (returning to the appropriateness of *equivocacy* to discussions of God), 'how common are Equivocal terms?': *'Is there a Divine on earth that will deny there are Equivocal terms in Scripture?'* Finally, he pleads, 'I pray you distinguish between Jesuitical dissembling Equivocation, and the *laudable yea necessary use of Equivocal words, when either the transcendencie of the matter,* the incapacity of men, the paucity of terms, the custom of speech, &c. hath made them *fit or needfull.'*[47]

What we need to understand before progressing any further, then, is that equivocation seems to have been an acceptable way of predicating the divine in seventeenth-century England: it replaced analogy, and it remained, for a while, anyway, a viable way of predicating the Being that is in God. Once we have accepted that fact, we are relieved and released into total enjoyment of Herbert's poetry, for we understand that it is *he*, the priest in 'The Church' (not his reader), who *breaks* the word and letter to expose the many which is one. This, finally, is transcendent language: the *one* word with *many* meanings, the *one* which contains *all.* Herbert is a ruthless equivocator; he rips language apart and dissects the word in order to reveal the one-all. Some of Herbert's most important equivocations are terms for his poetry itself. 'How shall I *measure* out thy bloud?' he asks in 'Good Friday': no man can 'quantify' the litres of lost blood reciprocally, but the priest-poet can 'measure' by verse. The *'lines'* of poetry, equivocally, are also the 'lines' to God: 'for life is straight / Straight as a *line,* that *ever tends to thee.'* 'Numbers' is another equivocated word for poetry: 'Shall I thy woes / *Number* according to thy foes.' Herbert's equivocations *make one* of the earthly-practicable and the heavenly-impracticable: it is possible to write a poem but it is difficult to climb to God. Equivocation logically joins the two tasks as one.

Much of Herbert's equivocal technique is concentrated in his art of 're-spelling' by substituting prefixes in significant words and, sometimes, removing prefixes altogether: this is, quite visibly, his *breaking* of the word. 'My deare, then I will *serve*,' he finally acquiesces in 'Love (III)'; but in the same poem, against the bareness of that word, are set more imperfect forms of the simplicity of that word: '*ob-serve*' ('quick-ey'd Love, *observing* me grow slack') and '*de-serve*' ('let my shame / Go where it doth *deserve*'). Imperfect spelling, notions of God as 'observing' and man 'deserving,' individuating words, keep man and God apart. Poetic 'de-*signes*' distract from God's own '*signes*,' and 'de-*lights*' (the 'sugred lies' and 'deceits' of 'The Rose') but mis-spell '*Light*': 'Then tell me, what is the supreme *delight*? / *Light*' ('Heaven'). Life which should 'tend' to God is mis-spelt 'ex-tend' at times and, worse yet, artistically, 'pre-tend' ('*How wide is all this long pretence*').

There is a very Herbertian remark in Edward Leigh's *Critica Sacra* which may indicate something of the spirit in which Herbert undertook to *spell* the word (making 'this' equal 'that' by the logic of equivocacy). Leigh derives 'Gospell' as '*Godspell*, the word of God, of *Ghosts spell*, the word of the Spirit': 'for *spell* in ancient time signified speech.'[48] But one need not turn to sources as obscure as Leigh to suggest that the art of equivocation might well have had Scriptural as well as logical origins. Augustine and a host of others *apologize* for the ambiguity and equivocacy of Scripture. While explaining something of the Anglican apologetic position that both Church and Scripture are 'subject to mistake' and must be interpreted in light of one another, Herbert Thorndike traces the fallibility of Scripture to the difficulty of the Greek and Hebrew, especially the Hebrew 'having originally no vowels to determine the reading of it, wanting conjunctions and prepositions to determine the signification of him that speaks.'[49] The 'manifold equivocations' which are incident to 'whatsoever is expressed by writing,' Thorndike explains, are exaggerated in Scripture by the authorial need to 'give us the sense of our Lord's words ... not the very syllables.' The 'words of our Saviour' registered in Holy Writ, Thorndike continues, 'are but in some sort an *imperfect and equivocal paraphrase* or expression of Christ's own true words, the *weakness of men's speech* and expression bearing no greater exactness.'[50] Of course, George Herbert's mentor, Lancelot Andrewes, was keenly interested in the examination of etymology and derivation in the interpretation of Scripture. Of his 'six means of interpretation' perhaps the most central is his '*Inspectio fontium*,' "to look to the original." '[51]

Unfortunately, it is very easy to see that Herbert is down on record in *The*

Country Parson (in 'The Parson preaching') as arguing that language should not be *broken*: 'The Parsons Method in handling of a text,' he maintains,

consists of two parts; first, a plain and evident declaration of the meaning of the text; and secondly, some choyce Observations drawn out of the whole text, as it lyes entire, and *unbroken* in Scripture it self. This he thinks naturall, and sweet, and grave. Whereas the other way of crumbling a text into small parts, as, the Person speaking, or spoken to, the subject, the object, and the like, hath neither sweetnesse, nor gravity, nor variety, since the words apart are not Scripture, but a dictionary, and may be considered alike in all the Scripture.

But there is a great difference between the activities of the 'Preacher' and the 'Priest' in 'The Church,' and whereas I would hardly deny that Herbert adopts the role of poet-preacher who concentrates on the *whole* text, I would also insist that he adopts the role of poet-priest who *breaks* the 'creature' of language and, thus, provides a 'dictionary' of the Word. Both poetically and theologically for Herbert his poet-priest role is the more *dignified* aspect of his dual function: 'The Countrey Parson being to administer the Sacraments, is at a stand with himself, how or what behaviour to assume for so holy things,' Herbert comments, 'Especially at Communion times he is in a great confusion, as being not only to receive God, but to *break*, and administer him.'[52] The wit required to 'break' the word is potentially lethal medicine: it is the 'poyson' of 'Assurance' ('what more / Could poyson, if it had a tongue, express?'), the poison of 'self love.' But the wit which originates as 'self love' in 'The Church' terminates in 'love and truth' ('What for it self love once began, / Now love and truth will end in man'): 'If all the hope and comfort that I gather' –

> Were from my self, I had not *half a word*,
> *Not half a letter* to oppose
> What is objected by my foes.

III HERBERT'S PREDICATION OF GOD

'Simplicity' is the major predicate for God in the poetry of George Herbert: God is One (and 'one-ly') and God is All ('Thy word is all'). To understand God's simplicity is to understand the logical paradox that One is All (and All is One), as well as to understand the linguistic paradox that the One is Many (equivocally) and that the Many is One (univocally). At the heart of the poet's understanding of his own function is his knowledge that 'Holy' is a *logical* homonym of 'Wholly' ('Heaven') and that to reach what is for 'Ever' he must 'per-*sever.*' Far from shying away from the predicates that are *unique* to God (simplicity, eternity, infiniteness), George Herbert bravely undertakes to deal in those unique predicates of God. He understands well the logical impropriety of 'de-fining' the 'in-finite' in the predication of God, and so he undertakes to 're-fine' the material of the predication of God in the 'fine-ness' of language itself: 'And if I please him, I write *fine* and wittie.' I think that Rosemond Tuve is right when she remarks that Herbert writes poetry like a theologian.[53] He shared many assumptions about the nature of God with St Thomas (his predicates), and he shared with Thomas a belief in the *need* to predicate God. But he rejected the most notable genres of St Thomas (the 'definitions,' 'curious questions and divisions' of 'Divinitie'), and he substituted equivocation for analogy in his own ontological system. Language, the 'is,' the 'being' in the *I AM* of God, is the stuff of ontology for Herbert, and for this reason he writes poetry. 'The Church' itself is Herbert's own logical 'middle term' which bridges the gap between words and their meaning in God, between 'terms' and the *I AM* of God.

Poetry's function, according to Herbert, is to lead to the '*All-heal*' of God (the 'All' which 'heals'): 'There is a balsome, or indeed a bloud, Dropping from heav'n, which doth cleanse and *close / All sorts of wounds*; of such strange force it is. / Seek out this *All-heal*' ('An Offering'). 'Division' is the mark of the Fall ('But all I fear is lest thy heart displease, / As neither good, nor *one*: so oft *divisions / Thy lusts have made*'), and 'Oneness' is the cure ('Thy passions also have their set partitions. / *These parcell out thy heart: recover* these, / And thou mayst offer *many gifts in one*'). According to Herbert in *The Country Parson*, the priest is also a physician ('The Countrey Parson desires to be all to his Parish, and not onely a Pastour, but Lawyer also, and a *Physician*'); the poet-priest applies what Augustine calls 'the medicine of Wisdom': 'healing some by contraries and some by similar things.'[54] The once 'fine' and 'seamlesse' coat of Wisdom, Herbert comments in 'Divinitie,' has been 'jagg'd': 'Then close again the seam, / Which thou hast open'd,' he concludes in 'The Size.' As poetry must stitch the seam and heal the wound of our division from the *I AM* of God, so it must 'close' the garden: 'Christ hath took a piece of ground, / And made a garden there for those / *Who want herbs for their wound.*'

'How shall I *measure*,' '*count*,' '*Number*,' '*score*'? The initial questions which Herbert asks about the nature of poetry in 'Good Friday' concern themselves with the Aristotelian 'predicament' of *quantity*. Quantities are either 'discrete or continuous,' Aristotle begins in the sixth chapter of his *Categories*, 'Of quantities that are *discrete* we may here instance *number and speech.'*[55] Measured in 'long and short syllables, speech is an evident quantity, whose parts possess no common boundary. No common limit exists, where those parts – that is, syllables – join. Each indeed, is distinct from the rest.' A 'line,' on the other hand, not 'discrete,' Aristotle explains, is 'continuous' quantity. In order to relate the One and the Many to the All, Herbert must cope with the predicament, 'quantity,' in his verse: in order to 'heal' he must render the 'discrete' as 'continuous.' He must turn 'syllable' into 'line' by making syllable resound in syllable homonymously, as 'this verse' marks 'that' in one *synonymous* and consonant Truth.

IV   PROLOGUE: A DECLENSION OF EQUIVOCACY

What follows is based on the assumption that for Herbert truth is located in the sound-consonancy of language itself expressed as the Name of God (I AM). The Name of God, linguistically speaking, is unique in that the subject-name is one and the same as the predicate and predication (I AM). All truth and beauty 'declines' from that name, and the duty of the poet is to reunite sounds homonymously in the one sound which *is* of God. The Babel myth, which is treated at some length by Herbert in a passage in his Latin poetry ('language being chaos since / The time of Babel'),[56] is at the centre of the story of Herbert's attitude toward language: it once *fell*, declined, from the *one* being of God, and the poet (or, such a poet as was Herbert) lives in constant danger of renewing the Babel event by diversifying rather than simplifying the One Name of God. Poetry (and, with it, the soul of the poet) is subject to 'Frailtie': 'It may a Babel prove / Commodious to conquer heav'n and thee / Planted in me.'

For the sake of offering a vocabulary with which to discuss the different kinds of equivocacy one encounters in the English poetry of George Herbert, I have collocated each of the five chapters which follow with a 'case' in a 'declension of equivocacy.' Chapter one, devoted to the 'Chirograph' (or idea of *writing*) in *The Temple*, I identify as *'nominative'* equivocacy. Writing (its numbers, measures, lines) is the central equivocal *subject* of *The Temple*; it invokes the idea of poet as namer (*nomino*-nominative) and is crucial, as we shall see, to the concept of the poet as priest. 'The Sacramental Voice,' or chapter two, I term *'genitive'* equivocacy because the equivocal phenomenon (thy voice-my voice, or, *my words-thy words*) is a matter of *possession*. The third chapter on ceremonies and Augustinianism, 'Use and Enjoyment,' I align with *'accusative'* equivocacy in that it is adverbial, indicating 'the goal or limit of an action that originates from the subject.'[57] The subject (as in, *I kneel*) becomes thus, equivocally, identified (*made one*) in its action with its object (God). 'Wisdom' (chapter four), I argue, can be discussed as *'dative'* equivocacy when the *image* of the second person of the Trinity (which is Wisdom) is *given* (*datus*-dative) by 'indirect implication in, or concern with, the action or state signified by the verb.' An interesting species of the dative case which is, I believe, bound up with the establishment of dative equivocacy is the so-called 'ethical dative' which indicates 'a certain emotional interest on the part of the person placed in the dative.' A dative relation is placed between the poet and Christ by the idea of Wisdom. Finally, in my last chapter on Anglicanism in Herbert's poetry, I discuss what I call *'ablative'* equivocacy because the ablative is instrumental in *locative* cases, because it can indicate 'source' (implying separation), because it can imply 'comparison,' and because it can be 'absolute' (suggesting accompaniment or *attendant circumstance*). The British Church, as Herbert states outright, is the *place* (location) of Beauty and Christ in this world and, as such, it is the *face* which God in Christ finally revealed to the world.

While I do not want to argue that Herbert himself consciously 'declined' equivocacy, I do want to stress that he was very consciously equivocal, rendering language itself the final locus and teleological focus of truth in the simplicity of God's Name. I would always argue the importance of grammar to the structure of thought in the seventeenth century,[58] but here I offer the notion of a 'declension' of equivocacy as a vocabulary, simply, for defining the varieties of equivocacy one encounters in the *The Temple* and for organizing the other concepts which attach themselves to the logical-theological function of equivocacy, 'Mans medley,' which is to *make one* ('both al/one') of heaven and earth.

1

The Chirograph: Liturgy and Ontology

I FAIR COPY

Profoundly significant, the references in *The Temple* to the poet's practice of the physical act of writing, to the *event* of his transcribing of the poem, have gone virtually unnoticed by modern criticism. The speaker begins his suggestion of this striking image pattern in 'The Thanksgiving,' there questioning how he can '*Copie*' Christ's '*fair, though bloudie hand*' ('how then shall I imitate thee, and / *Copie thy fair, though bloudie hand*?'). His concern continues, and while considering the potential hazards implicit in the 'false embroyderies' of the traditional materials of poetry in 'Vanitie (II),' the speaker cautions himself, 'Heark and beware, lest what you now do measure / And *write* for sweet, prove a most sowre displeasure.'[1] But, more than any other poem, 'Assurance' demonstrates not just the existence but the *meaning* of this extremely self-conscious preoccupation of the poet's. Here the speaker makes the *act* of handwriting a *re-enactment* of Christ's death on the Cross, 'Thou art not only to perform thy part, / But also mine':

> *Thou didst at once thy self indite,*
> *And hold my hand, while I did write.*

For George Herbert the writing of poetry or, more specifically, the *act or ceremony* of writing a poem, connects itself in the eternal scheme of things (where events recapitulate themselves by liturgical expression and representation) with the *event* on the Cross. Christ *indites himself* in the poem, participating in the transcription with his own 'bloudie hand.' The poet's chirograph, then, is endowed with ontological significance and becomes a meaningful re-enactment of the primordial meaning of Good Friday, equivocating the two events: poet's writing and Christ's dying. As Herbert observes in his poem entitled 'Good Friday,'

> *Since bloud is fittest, Lord, to write*
> *Thy sorrows in,* and bloudie fight;
> My heart hath store, write there, where in
> One box doth lie both *ink and sinne.*

Poems outside the body of *The Temple* reveal something of the same obsession that *The Temple* does with the scribal act of copying the poem and entrusting it to paper, pen, and ink.[2] 'Sure, Lord, there is enough in thee to dry / Oceans of Ink,' Herbert writes in the second of the sonnets sent to his mother. The poem 'To Melville' in the 'Musae Responsoriae' also reveals a concern with the 'hand' which writes the poems to which Herbert is responding and the 'noble right hands' which draw up the 'signature' of the poem. Of all the poems outside *The Temple*, however, it is a poem in the 'Passio Discerpta' which renders the meaning of the poet's chirograph in terms which most resemble the chirograph in *The Temple*. Appropriately, it is generated from the same *topos* that becomes identified with the act of writing in *The Temple*, 'To the dying Lord':

> Since so much wounding overcomes my eyes, my tears,
> I will have no effect, though melted down in weeping.
> *Let ink help me out,*
> *A liquid more akin to guilt;*
> Let my *sins, now tinted right, pour forth their tears.*

What *differs* about this chirograph and the chirograph of *The Temple* is plain enough: the ink is black (for sin) rather than red (for 'bloudie hand') even though, once again, the *act* of writing is the gesture of repentance which is to be made operative by the Cross. Here, in the 'Passio Discerpta' (out of the context of 'The Church') the judgment against sin does not turn into Christ's own judgment against himself: the ink remains black rather than red – it has not yet achieved the status of the Sacrament's *blood which was shed for guilty man.*

Before concentrating exclusively on the text of *The Temple* to examine the implications of Herbert's many invocations of the image of his own pen inscribing, we do well to consider the diverse tradition out of which such a concern must have sprung: it is in this context that we must consider Herbert's own use of that tradition. Sidney and Shakespeare before him had, of course, provided some precedent for Herbert's self-conscious concern with the meaning of the holding of his pen. And the pen as sword was a standard Renaissance trope to be found especially in the emblem books on the continent, expressing an idea not uncongenial to Herbert that 'writing is discovery and victory.'[3] But the tradition in which Herbert is working is paradoxical (writing can turn against itself into a 'sowre displeasure') and that paradox is to be found not in profane but in Biblical and religious tradition. Christ's entire life on earth, as it is portrayed by the writers of the Gospels in the New Testament, is set against and in opposition to the legalism of the Scribes of the Old Testament. All that Christ preaches undoes the slavish *copying* of the Law: 'For he taught them as one having authority, and not as the scribes' (Matthew 7:29). In spite of the fact that it found no institution in the life of Christ, however, the scribal art by the sixth century had found a passionate spokesman in the person of the scholar and monk, Cassiodorus, who returned to the Old Testament for his defence. 'I admit that among those of your tasks which require physical effort, that of the scribe, if he writes correctly, appeals most to me,' Cassiodorus argues in his *Institutiones Divinarum et Saecularium Litterarum*. Explaining that with a 'gliding pen the heavenly words are copied so that the devil's craft ... may be destroyed' and, invoking Old Testament attitudes toward the scribal effort by stating that scribes 'deserve praise too for seeming in some way to *imitate* the action of the Lord, who, though it was expressed figuratively, wrote His law with the use of His all-powerful finger' (Exodus 31:18), Cassiodorus eulogizes the exercise of handwriting as a form of worship:

Happy his design, praiseworthy his zeal, to *preach to men with the hand alone*, to open tongues with fingers, to give salvation silently to mortal, and to fight against the illicit temptations of the devil with *pen and ink.*[4]

Transcription, chirography, is for Cassiodorus an act of Christian warfare recording, and later for Herbert *representing*, the fight against the devil; but it is for Herbert an act not without complexities.

To come straight to the point: because it is a *legal* act grounded on ideas of Jewish *ceremony and merit* (pitting itself against the 'illicit' work of the devil), the handwriting exercise identifies itself with the written *letter of the law* which kills, according to Paul, and which, through Christ, has been replaced by the 'spirit' which gives life (2 Corinthians 3:6). The original polarity between the attitudes of the Old Testament and the New toward the use of ceremony in worship (controlling the attitudes toward the ceremoniousness of chirography) reawakens in the conflicting convictions about ceremony in

Reformation England. A great deal can be learned by observing the range of interpretations of a text which became in sixteenth- and seventeenth-century England a *locus classicus* for the Puritan abolition of ceremony in worship: Colossians 2:14, where Christ is described as 'Blotting out the *handwriting* of ordinances that was against us, which was contrary to us, and took it out of the way, nailing it to his cross.' N. Byfield, with rather reductive Puritanism, in 1617 interprets the handwriting as the debt which was driving into bankruptcy the ceremonial law and which Christ abolished on the Cross. 'If the ceremonies were a *Chyrographe*,' he maintains in opposition to the Church of England's judicious maintenance of *some* Roman ceremonies, 'or *handwriting against us*, and Christ hath removed them by fastening them upon the crosse, therefore we ought not to receive them again.'[5] Calvin too, before Byfield, had interpreted the 'handwritinges,' 'rites,' and 'ceremonies' as 'shewes of mens guiltinesse': 'ceremonies themselves didde seale up and signe guiltinesse.'[6] The potential danger in continuing with the dispensation of the law under the ordinance of handwriting is most succinctly summarized by Lancelot Ridley in 1548: 'it pleaseth God of his mercie, not onely to forgeue us our synnes, but also *to take awaie that hande writyng, that condempneth us for synn to deth and that writyng was the lawe of God written.*'[7]

But Herbert was no Puritan: his close association with the Ferrar family, his statements about the need for ceremony in worship in both the 'Musae Responsoriae' and *The Country Parson*, and the numerous references to gestures, postures, vestments, and set prayers in *The Temple* themselves align him with the extremely decorous, perhaps even what would a decade later be called Laudian, element in the Church of England.[8] In brief, Herbert believed *to some extent* in the validity of ceremony, perhaps even more so than Donne, but he held fast to what he himself called the *via media* of Anglicanism. To King James he writes, 'you endure / with greater confidence as Puritans / and Roman Catholics arouse the waves / Between which / you, the Shepherd, drive your sheep, / Safest in a *via media*.' Not believing with the Puritans in the total abolition of the ordinance of handwriting (the ceremonies and 'shows' of man's guiltiness), he nevertheless believed, as he tells us in his notes on Valdesso's *Considerations*, that 'at least some of the Papists are come now, to what the Pharisees were come in our Saviours time.'

Herbert's criteria for weeding out the valid from the invalid ceremonies in the ordinance of handwriting are traditional enough. Those are invalid which are 'super-induced to the scriptures.'[9] Those ceremonies are kept (in the twenty-fifth article of the Church of England) which are '*Sacraments* ordained of Christ our Lord in the Gospel.' Ceremony becomes sacrament when it is not 'gazed upon' but *used* to the point of 'a wholesome *effect or operation*,' to continue in the terms of the Church's 'Of the Sacraments.' Chirography for Herbert in 'The Church' is just such a ceremony-become-sacrament, an *efficacious sign* and *rehearsal* of the event on the Cross. As such, it is not just the single fight of a solitary man against sin but an imitation and representation of Good Friday's 'bloudie fight.' The oneness of the act of writing and the event of the Cross is further stressed by the concluding realization in 'Good Friday' that (conversely), should sin win the fight, there would be no poem: 'oh fill the place, / ... Lest sinne take courage and return, / And *all the writings blot or burn.*' Poetry is an efficacious sign of Christ's *victory* on the Cross and is, as such, a rewriting of the former handwriting 'which is against us.'

Herbert understands his writing as an act of predication. 'O let me still,' he pleads in 'H. Baptisme (II),' ' *Write* thee great God, and me a childe.' To *write* is to lay claim on what *is* (and what *was* and *will be*) in the eternal *being* of God. Writing transcends itself in 'The Church': as in 'Obedience' words become 'Deed,' both deed-act and a deed of real-estate to the speaker's heart. On the paper which conveys 'a Lordship' the poet 'writes' his heart, spills the ink-blood of his heart: 'On it my heart doth bleed / As many lines, as there doth need / To passe it self and all it hath to thee.' But Herbert never forgets the sensitivity of his sacramental gauge, the potential hazard of his writing, which can *accuse* (and once did) as well as *excuse* him sacramentally in Christ. What he now *writes* for sweet may prove 'a most sowre displeasure' when writing ceases to be sacrament and retains only the guiltiness of 'show.' In its very nature the poetry is paradoxical, condemning at the same time that it saves: it is written against itself, and Christ indites himself to suffering under the hands of the Law in the *event* of the poem.

Enough cannot be said about the fact that it is Herbert's Anglicanism that allows him the flexibility to see both sides of the story, both Old Testament and New, both Catholic and Puritan, in his interpretation of the meaning of the handwriting which, according to the Puritans, serves only to condemn us to guiltiness once more. Donne, who absorbed more Puritanism than did Herbert, has a useful explication of the condemnation implicit in the ' *Chirographum*' in a sermon on James 2:12 delivered in February, 1628:

But yet there is worse evidence against me, then either this *Chirographum*, the first hand-writing of *Adams* hand, or then this *pactum*, this contract of mine own hand, actuall and habituall sin (for of these, one is wash'd out in water, and the other in blood, in the two Sacraments.) But then there is *Lex in Membris* ... relapses into repented sin. [10]

This '*Lex in membris*,' not washed away by the sacraments of water and of blood, is finally, according to Donne, 'beaten back, as a tide by a bank, by a continual opposing the merits and example of Christ Jesus.' That *beating back*, for Herbert anyway, is the spiritual exercise of poetry where *Christ holds the pen* while he writes.

In an undated sermon on Lamentations 3:1, Donne digresses to the Colossians text about the handwriting once again, and he defies the Puritan interpretation of it; he articulates a *via media* Anglican position about that Chirograph: 'the death of Christ is given to us, as a *Handwriting*,' he argues, 'for, when Christ nail'd that Chirographum, that first hand-writing, that had passed between the Devill and us, to his Crosse, *he did not leave us out of debt*, nor absolutely discharged, but he laid another *Chirographum* upon us, *another Obligation arising out of his death*.'[11] Far from interpreting the text as an injunction against the handwriting which had been identified with the ceremonies of the Law, Donne here turns the passage into an injunction to continue with the writing and to do as Herbert does in *copying* the 'fair' and 'bloudie' hand of his Lord. Christ's death, Donne continues, delivered to us '*as a writing*' is given 'in the nature of *a Copy*, to learne by': 'It is not onely given us to reade, but *to write over*, and practice.'

In short, whereas to the Puritan the handwriting implies Adam's pact with the devil, to the Anglican it means *both* Adam's chirograph and Christ's death on the cross *at once*. Language for the Anglican poet is a tool which acquaints man at once with his fall in Adam and his Redemption on the Cross. While ultimately redemptive, writing begins by emphasizing earthliness: it is 'the good fellowship of dust.' Earthbound, the 'dustie' lines of poetry become, nevertheless, as in 'Church-monuments,' the 'school' where flesh learns to '*spell* his elements, and finde his birth / *Written*' in the 'heraldrie and *lines*.' Even the most Laudian Anglican of the time accepts a modicum of the reformed attitude toward the handwriting. And it would seem that thus, for Herbert, writing remains irrevocably a reminder of the guiltiness of man as original sinner, who in 'The Sinner' pleads pharisaically and legally, renewing the handwriting of the Law: '*Remember that thou once didst write in stone*.' In an interesting earlier version of 'Good Friday' in the Williams MS, Herbert concludes with an image of his writing as Adam's chirograph: 'for by the writings all may see / Thou hast an ancient claim to me.' But the earlier images of the sinfulness of the writing are revoked as the poet lays claim to the merits and example of Christ by but copying *his* writing. It is by copying rather than by inventing that the poet can save the 'expense' of sin which disrupts the economy of the Creation, as he learns in 'Jordan (II)': 'There is in *love* a sweetnesse readie penn'd: / *Copie* out onely that, and save *expense*.' Not so much a pious word (in the texture of poetry itself) as a *logical* word denoting relation, the word 'love' explains the phenomenological union of subject and object, soul and Christ, in the 'sign' of the poet's language. Language-Logos is 'that love' first 'expressed' and 'disclosed' on the Cross, now 'measured,' reconciling the distance between the poet and Christ by the unity of equivocation: as the poet 'measures' his verse, Christ 'measures' his blood. Now expressed as equi-vocation (calling one), love *makes one* of the writing of a single man and the bloody writing of his Lord.

Crucial to the distinction between guilty ceremony and efficacious sacrament is the poet's intention and purpose in the act of writing the poem. The ceremony of handwriting cannot *merit*, as does the Law, or make a legal claim against the debt of Adam's chirograph on the basis of its own self-righteousness. Poetry cannot *pay back* by its ceremony; equivocally, however, it can 'measure out' the price already paid in 'Good Friday.' It can '*count* what thee befell' not by accounting but by re-counting, and it can 'number' woes not arithmetically ('For though I die for thee, *I am behinde* / My sinnes deserve the condemnation') but in the numbers of verse. Legal ceremony works against itself to bankrupt the accounts, and the principle of individual enterprise leads to an unhealthy economy of strictly accounted writing whose futility Herbert describes in 'Praise (1)': 'To *write* a verse or two is all the praise, / That I can raise: / *Mend my estate.*' Overcome by the writing on the Cross in 'The Crosse,' the poet complains that his ceremonious chirograph, his 'power to *serve*,' has been taken away; Christ unbends, he observes, 'All my abilities, my *designes* confound.' Christ undoes the Adamic art of the poet's handwriting and lays his '*threatnings* bleeding on the ground.' The legal 'threatnings' of artistic merit, of the poet's own chirograph, are brought low and made to 'bleed' in the handwriting of his Lord nailed to the Cross, where *merit* is not his own. Here ceremony becomes sacrament as the poet's words ('but foure words, *my words*') lay claim to Christ's words ('*Thy will be done*'), and the 'show' of the chirograph becomes 'sign' when the poet recalls the event which the chirograph celebrates and *in which it participates.*

When writing gives up its claim as original (in which it is Adam's chirograph) and accepts its identity as *copy* (by which it is Christ's handwriting delivered to be *written over again*), it defines itself as 'A true Hymne' where Christ completes the poet's act, transforming the chirograph from *becoming* into *being*: 'As when th'heart sayes (sighing to be approved) / O, *could I love!* and stops: *God writeth, Loved.*' In the sacramental chirograph Herbert finds a method which leads him beyond the 'false embroyderies' of a poem to the *life* which is 'hid with Christ in God.' In 'The Flower' Herbert summarizes his spiritual journey in language itself, his journey from Adam's chirograph (which *spells* death) to Christ's handwriting on the Cross (which *is* his life): 'After so many *deaths* I *live and write.*' Such writing engages all that *is*, for it takes part in the pure *being* of God, and, hence, 'We say amisse, / This or that *is*: / Thy word *is all*, if we could spell.'

II INK AND THE SPIRIT

When E.D. Hirsch speaks of 'intrinsic genre,' he provides a very useful tool for coping with the hermeneutic difficulties of the discrepancy between apparent form and authorial intent which exist in *The Temple*.[12] *Psalm*, a poem of prayer and praise, is what *The Temple* appears to be; but behind the smooth surface of the poem 'intrinsic genre' struggles in the two extremes of an equivocated word: *the letter*. 'Letters' in *The Temple* are both the *letters of the law* (engraved in stone-paper) and the *living letters of the spirit*, and the *letters* of a poem in *The Temple* can operate either as 'the ministration of *death*, written and engraven in stones' (2 Corinthians 3:7) or as the *embodied letter* of the Corinthians '*written in our hearts*' (2 Corinthians 3:2): 'ye are manifestly declared to be the *epistle of Christ*,' St. Paul writes the Corinthians, 'ministered by us, *written not with ink* but *with the Spirit of the living God*; not in tables of stone, but in the fleshly tables of the heart' (3:3). Expressing in its equivocacy (something 'written' and something 'sent') the full complexity of Herbert's religious language, the 'letter' bridges the gulf between the text and the living God.

According to Chrysostom (the fourth-century 'golden-mouthed' Bishop whom Walton identifies with Herbert), Paul in this passage from Corinthians 'cuts at the root of the Jewish arrogancy. For the *Law* and *nothing else but letters* ... but pillars and *writings bearing death* to those who transgress the letters.' A seventeenth-century Puritan such as David Dickson writing in 1659 finds in this passage a total opposition between 'ink' and 'spirit,' between 'stone' and 'heart,' between 'works' (the written Letter) and 'grace' (given in the New Covenant):

The Ministry of the Law, or the Covenant of Works is onely the Letter written or spoken, *without efficacy*, without all spiritual virtue to perform that which it commands: But the Ministry of the Gospel, or the Covenant of Grace through Christ, is the Ministering of the Spirit, because, according to, and by that, the Holy Ghost is administered, whereby the hearer is quickened and strengthened to embrace that which is propounded.[13]

Herbert, on the other hand, does not make such a rigid distinction between the labour of the 'letter' (the ceremonies, the handwriting inscribed with ink on paper or engraved in tables of stone) and the 'spirit' (whose territory is heaven-heart). For Herbert (and here I return to the language of the twenty-fifth Article), the ink, the letter, and the stone can become '*effectual signs of grace.*' The 'letter' of the Jews (and of their 'analogat,' the Papists, as Herbert calls them in *Valdesso*) for an Anglican is related *sacramentally* to the operation of the Spirit, and in sacrament what was once a contradiction becomes an *effective sign.* This is not to say by any means that for Herbert the 'letter' could not damn to the ministration of death as well as signify. Quite the contrary: *The Temple* records the spiritual-artistic journey to an understanding of the letter and ink *as sign.* It is a struggle which resolves paradoxes by *accommodating* the ink to the spirit and *accommodating* the writing of the poem to the writing in the heart. Nothing could be more clear than the original difficulty Herbert has in relating the letter *written in ink and engraved in stone* to the heart which is that stone in 'Sepulchre,' the stone where Christ lies dead, uninanimated: 'And as of old the Law by heav'nly art / Was writ in stone; so thou, which also art / The *letter of the word*, find'st no fit heart / To hold thee.' When it is an end in itself rather than a means to the Spirit, the ink and the handwriting of the poem remain in a place where Christ is to be found dead. And the letters of the poem, stones which 'in quiet entertain thee,' do not convey the Word but hide it in the 'letter of the word.'[14] Hermeneutics here are static, and the handwriting is an icon retaining its own interpretation. Such writing does not participate sacramentally in the moment Christ indites himself on the Cross, but it ministers death, judgment, and damnation to its faithless participants. The stones themselves cannot be 'indited' for murder, the speaker tells us, but we ourselves – 'our hard hearts have took up stones to brain thee.' Stony hearts, which receive the sacrament without 'wholesome effect or operation,' the Church's twenty-fifth Article warns, 'purchase to themselves damnation.'

Within the two senses of the one word, 'letter,' Herbert finds a statement of the significance of his writing as *both* in ink and of the Spirit. His 'letters' are both inscribed after the manner of the Law and sent after the manner of St Paul's epistles. Herbert does not pun to confound but to unfold the mysterious truth. In 'The British Church' the letters are both *fixed* (as in the stone of the Church) and *sent* (as a missive to the human heart). In the 'perfect lineaments' of the properly proportioned *via media* of Anglicanism, 'Beautie' takes up her place, 'And *dates her letters* from thy face, / When she doth *write.*' Like Donne's, Herbert's verse has the 'middle nature' of Anglicanism, creating commerce between Heaven and Earth, in equivocated language. The entire group of poems entitled 'The Church' is the place both *on which* beauty writes and *from which* she sends her living epistles to human hearts. Language itself in *The Temple* is the 'face' on which the letters of the Spirit are written; and it is a 'glass' where we 'with open *face*' behold the glory of God and 'are *changed into the same image*' (2 Corinthians 3:18).

'Love-joy,' which both discusses and acts out the implications of the letter engraved (here 'anneal'd') as *sign*, is actually set against the back-drop of that glass (or window) which, to Paul, Augustine, and others, represents the *enigma* that characterizes all sight of God in this life (1 Corinthians 13:12):

> As on a window late I cast mine eye,
> I saw a vine drop grapes with *J* and *C*
> Anneal'd on every bunch.

After remarking that the spectacle seems to be 'the *bodie* and the *letters* both / Of *Joy* and *Charitie*,' the speaker is told of his interpretive success: 'It figures JESUS CHRIST.' In the tradition in which Herbert is writing, written letters are the body of Christ ('the bodie and the letters both'). Poetic language inhabits the ontological distance between the ink, the heart, and Christ himself, joining them as one. 'Sepulchre,' which works similarly to identify Christ's body and the letter ('O blessed bodie! Whither art thou thrown?') indeed argues rather discouragingly at the outset of *The Temple* that there is but one place for the body-letter: on the stone-page of the printed word which reflects the stone-heart of the unresponsive reader. But in 'Love-joy' the heart finds a place for those letters, and Christ is once again found alive in the glass and face of language. The 'grapes' on which the letters of language are annealed in 'Love-joy' are the grapes which will become the sacramental wine of Word. Even the 'Divine Word' may be understood by the grape, Augustine observes in a suggestive passage from his *Commentary on the Psalms*:

when the Divine Word maketh use of, by necessity of declaring Himself, the sound of the voice, whereby to convey Himself to the ears of the hearers; in the same sound of the voice, as it were in husks, knowledge, like the wine, is enclosed: and so this grape comes into the ears, as into the pressing machines of the winepressers.[15]

'*As into the pressing machines*': the 'pressing machine' for the grape of the letter (and external voice) in Herbert's poetry is his *modus operandi* of anatomizing the letter, of carving, serving, and *pressing* it for significance. He spells, crumbles, and *crushes* the letter. Like the Pomanders and wood of 'The Banquet,' language is *broken* eucharistically ('God, to show how farre his love / Could improve, / Here, as *broken* is presented') and, 'being bruis'd,' is 'better sented' (equivocally, scented-sented). As Herbert himself puts it in 'The Priesthood,' his carving and crushing of the letter renders his lay-sword the holy word (s/word). In 'Paradise' the letter is pruned ('Such cuttings rather *heal than* REND'), 'When thou dost greater judgements SPARE, / And with thy knife but prune and PARE, / Ev'n fruitfull trees more fruitfull ARE.' And an anatomy of the name of the Mother of God ('Mary') brings forth the *Lord of Hosts* 'Army'). Pressed and carved by the knife of the poem, the written word is the basis of Herbert's epistemology: by anatomizing the 'bodie' and 'letter' Herbert comes into knowledge of the presence of his God in words, the flesh in which Christ pitches his tent. Like the words '*My Master*' in 'The Odour,' language in *The Temple* grows into 'a sweet content' (both meaning and satisfaction): it 'leaves a rich *sent.*' What is 'sent' is reflective participation in the Wisdom and understanding of the 'Master': 'Then should the *Pomander*, which was before / A *speaking sweet, mend by reflection,* / And *tell me more.*'

The *Pomander* (*pomme d'ambre*), the 'speaking sweet' *apple* of language itself in both 'The Odour' and 'The Banquet,' is both the apple of which Adam ate and the apple which must now be 'pared' by the knife of poetry. 'Pick out of tales the mirth, but not the sinne,' Herbert warns in 'The Church-porch': '*He pares his apple,* that will cleanly feed.' Language acts out for Herbert the ultimate theological paradox of the damning-saving 'letter': 'For as in Adam all die, even so in Christ shall all be made alive' (1 Corinthians 15:22). Christ hangs in 'The Sacrifice' charged with 'a world of sinne' which 'came in / By *words.*' But the 'Pomanders and wood' of the tree-Cross (the words which when '*bruised*' are better scented) are the seed which will *bruise* the head of the serpent (Genesis 3:15). 'Look to thy mouth; diseases enter there,' Herbert comments in the idiom of the natural man in 'The Church-porch': 'if thy stomack call; / *Carve, or discourse*; do not a famine fear.' Carving, the cutting and splicing of the letter of the word in 'The Church,' is an act which represents New Testament man's resistance to the literalism-sensousness (the stomack's call) of the letter of the law (man's hunger in the manner of the first Adam after the readily enjoyed but thus-aborted meaning in God's universe). The equivocation which results from such anatomies of the letter is troublesome to the niggardly legality of the Old Man alone, for it is he alone who cannot interpret beyond the outwardness of the 'J' and 'C' to see *both* the meaning and the figure, and to see that signs are not one thing *or* another but one thing *and* another in the economy of God's continuing presence and self-signification in providential history.

Herbert's poetic world has a solidity to it; it is a verbal icon which does not collapse totally into the *applica* of Puritan hermeneutics. The dynamics of meaning in *The Temple* are not so much that the 'lines' of poetry must reach the 'heart' as that the 'heart' must reach the 'lines,' as Herbert indicates in both 'A true Hymn' ('when the soul *unto the lines accords*') and 'Obedience' ('If some kinde man would thrust his heart / *Into these lines*'). The poem itself retains what some have thought was lost by seventeenth-century England: ontological value. The poem's function is both to mean *and* be; and, as Herbert indicates in 'The Banquet,' the poem's destiny is in that Being without which nothing else is: 'Let the wonder of his pitie / Be my dittie, / And *take up my lines and life.*' Blood-handwriting and stone-letters, the iconography of this verbal icon, are interpreted by the poet-as-priest to mediate between the icon and God. Herbert's Anglicanism inclines him to adopt both roles: poet-preacher and poet-priest. In the final analysis, Herbert's verbal icon works as an ontological bridge, re-spelling the universe, and re-integrating the individuating language (which defines things separately) into oneness which is the Being of God. Herbert's 'apology' for spelling in 'The Flower' is an extension of his well-annotated notion that what poetry does is to search for truth (what *is*). Language is broken in *The Temple*, and the breaking of the *letters* of the word (in 'discovery') uncovers what is 'amisse' and allows the possibility of escaping the limitations of a tool which otherwise confuses that '*is.*'

III POETRY AND ECHO

'Heaven' furnishes us with Herbert's own comment on the ontological domain of the poetry of *The Temple*: poetry *echoes* between heaven and earth. Originating in the 'leaves' (holy leaves) of Holy Scripture, poetry echoes in the vitality of the present, interpreting and adjusting that meaning *now*, at the same time that it prefigures the totality and perfection (wholly) of the 'delights on high.' 'The Scriptures are Gods Voyce,' John Donne remarks in a sermon which illuminates Herbert's Echo poem, '*The Church is his Eccho*; a redoubling, a repeating of some particular syllables, and accents of the same voice.'[16] What is said by Donne about the Church as the Echo of Scripture holds true for Herbert's 'Church': it is a volume of poetry which redoubles some partial sounds (wholly-holy) of the voice of God heard in Scripture. And that echo is heard as the pared letter (high-I) of the poetic word. Renaissance mythographers take an almost universal interest in the figure of Echo because of her relationship with Pan, and Francis Bacon identifies her explicitly as Syrinx, or *writing*, who is held to transcribe (echo) 'Exactly as Nature dictates.'[17] As she is 'genuine philosophy' to Bacon, so she is 'genuine theology' to Herbert: Herbert's poetry is his method of reflecting on things divine, resounding the Word of God by striking the individual notes which become God's harmony, the 'three parts vied/And multiplied' which *im-part* the consonancy of wholly-holy.

For Herbert poetry is echo because it is a partial testimony not *of* but *in* the Word *now*. 'In Scriptures you have *Praeceptum*, the thing it self, What; In the Church, you have the *Nunc*, the time, When,' Donne says of the echo of Scripture in the Church,

> And as we hearken with earnestnesse, and some admiration at an Eccho, when per-chance we doe not understand the voice which occasioned that Eccho; so doe the obedient children of God apply themselves to the Eccho of his Church, when per-chance otherwise, they would lesse understand the voice of God, in his Scriptures, if that voice were not so redoubled unto them.[18]

Just such a notion of Scripture as *Praeceptum* and the Church as *Nunc* ac-tually structures the argument of Herbert's poem entitled 'Lent': 'The Scrip-tures bid us *fast*; the Church sayes, *now*.' In short, Scriptures give the *what* (precept) and the Church the *when*. And although the interpretation *in time* of the Word-precept-What falls short of its eternal truth, 'Yet to go part of that religious way,' Herbert maintains, 'Is better then to rest': 'We cannot reach our Saviours puritie; / Yet are we bid, *Be holy ev'n as he.*' Text echoes as the spirit *now*, however weakly: Heaven, Scripture, Church, poem, and the *now* of Herbert's reader arrange meaning vertically on the ontological chain of being which hangs on the Word itself, 'for in ev'ry thing / Thy words to finde me out, & parallels bring, / And in another make me understood.'

According to John Chrysostom, the major *difference* between the letters of the Law and the living epistles of the Spirit is a matter of *place*: 'the Law was *fixed in one place*; not as the Spirit, was *present in all places*, breathing great might into all.'[19] The accomplishment of Herbert's poetry rests in the fact that what it *is* (the Body of Christ) is paradoxically both present in all places and fixed in one place at once: heaven, church, heart, and the 'face' of the poem are identified (*made one*) on the surface of language itself as Beauty *takes up a place* in the very letter of the poem. Church bells are heard beyond the stars ('Prayer I'), and although 'The earth is not too low' that 'praises there may grow,' so neither are the heavens too high: 'His praise may thither flie' ('Antiphon I'). In defining all 'contraries,' Aristotle observes in his *Cate-gories*, we seem to have *space* in mind: 'For we call those things contrary which, being also within the same class, are *most distant* the one from the other.'[20] As priest, Herbert reconciles those distant contraries in the materials of the creative Word, or *Logos*. He *celebrates* an eternal moment which is recorded in heaven, heart, and stars: he remembers the Word and its price, Christ's blood, and he recreates its presence in time. Language for Herbert is the *way* to heaven; it is the *way* 'Home': 'What have I left, that I should stay and grone? / *The most of me to heav'n is fled.*' The heart's pilgrimage to heaven *via* language can be accomplished in the renewal of the *praeceptum* (Word) of Scriptures: 'heav'n lies flat in thee,' Herbert observes of 'The H. Scriptures,' 'Subject to ev'ry mounters *bended knee.*' The 'bended knee' is, of course, the gesture of prayer and the 'crouch' of 'Antiphon (II)' ('*Ang.* We adore. / *Men.* And we do crouch'), and it is this gesture which finally *makes one* of the heaven and earth which the poem echoes between: 'Praised be the God alone, / Who hath made of *two folds one.*' The poetry of prayer is, as Herbert represents it, precarious poetry which holds perilous balance: 'With one small sigh thou gav'st me th'other day / I blasted all the joyes about me.' The great ontological *reach* of the poem's meaning reflects itself in the surface tension of language: 'take me up to thee,' Herbert appeals in 'Home' –

> My flesh and bones and joynts do pray:
> *And ev'n my verse*, when by the ryme and reason
> The word is, *Stay*, sayes ever, *Come*.

What his 'verse' records, the paradox of the near-distance between heaven and earth (*stay-come*), the poem and its echo, is a theme which Herbert pursues explicitly from the very start of *The Temple*. After seeking his 'rich Lord' in heaven 'at his manour,' the speaker of 'Redemption' travels to earth looking in great resorts, cities, theatres, courts. He finds him dying on the Cross. 'Where is my God? what hidden place / Conceals thee still?' Herbert asks in 'The Search': 'My knees pierce th'*earth*, mine eies the *skie*.' The search for the *place* of God (what Donne repeatedly calls in his sermons the *ubi* of God) is a problem which is very much an issue of topical interest in seventeenth-century Anglican writing because of its close relationship to the heated debate about the Real Presence of Christ in the chief sacrament, the Lord's Supper. They of 'the Roman Perswasion,' Donne complains in a sermon while discussing the *image* of God, 'come too neare to giving God a body ... too neare in their Transubstantiation ... too neare to our sense.' God's presence in the Sacrament, Donne continues, is, on the other hand, 'not too neare our faith':

not too neare in the *Ubi*; for so it is there: There, that is, in that place to which the Sacrament extends it selfe. For *the Sacrament extends as well to heaven*, from whence it fetches grace, as to the table, from whence it delivers the Bread and Wine.[21]

Of the place, the *Ubi*, where God is to be found, Donne comments further in another sermon, 'the Church, which is his Vineyard, is his *Ubi*, his place, his Center': 'in the Church, in the Sermon, in the Sacrament he returns to us.'[22] On *earth* God finds his place, Donne argues, 'he returns to me as to his Earth, that Earth which he hath made his by assuming my nature, I am become his *Ubi*, his place' ('though in the dayes of my sinne, God hath absented himselfe from me').[23] For Herbert the search for the *Ubi* of God is a more difficult one than it is for Donne, at least apparently so: in 'The Crosse' he sighs, seeks, faints, dies, 'Untill I had some *place*, where I might sing.' 'My searches are my *daily bread*; / Yet never *prove*,' Herbert complains of the difficulty in finding the sacramental *locus* of his poetry (that which will 'extend' and 'echo' between heaven and earth). The 'distance' is both vast and null, for the problem in bringing together heaven and earth is neither in space nor time itself but in language which defies the limits of space and time: 'as thy absence doth excell / All distance known: / So doth thy nearnesse bear the bell, / *Making two one.*' *Two makes one* on the equivocal surface of language where, homonymously, two words sound as one. Sacramentally, then, language, which can unite *as one* both heaven and earth and bridge the distance between them, can also, on its own (as mere 'creature'), like Babel grow, 'Commodious to conquer *heav'n and thee* / Planted *in me.*'

In a sense, by bridging the gulf between Puritanism and Roman Catholicism, George Herbert's *via media* Anglicanism also overcomes the theological division between heaven and earth as the *Ubi* for God. Verse, another form of 'his image' for the seventeenth-century Anglican, compromised the Roman earth (too near) with the Separatist heaven unrelated to earth. The Anglican aesthetic 'echoes' through the middle territory between ink and the spirit. And seventeenth-century responses to the poetry of George Herbert suggest that in Herbert's artistic version of the Anglican compromise both Puritan and Roman Catholic saw what they wanted. Richard Crashaw's Catholicism, for instance, inclines him to respond to Herbert's book as icon in 'On Mr. G. *Herberts* booke intituled the Temple of Sacred Poems, sent to a Gentlewoman' and to place the icon, in sacramental gesture, on the 'shrine' of a lady's 'white hand.'[24] But Richard Baxter's Puritanism (and Puritan audience) renders him susceptible to the 'Spirit' of Herbert's language: '*Heart-work* and *Heaven-work* make up his Books,'[25] Baxter comments about the poetry of Herbert. In general, the Puritan emphasis on the heart and heaven as the *Ubi* of God precludes an ability to see the participation of the letter, the ink, the handwriting, in the *total* (wholly-holy) meaning of Herbert's poetry. And it eliminates the tension and paradox of the poetry. Herbert 'speaks *to* God,' Baxter argues (simplifying Herbert); Herbert's business in the world 'is most *with God.*'[26] But to make God the sole audience of Herbert's poetry is to misread Herbert's own intention, which is to speak *both* to man and to God, *both* on earth and in heaven.

Frequently the debate about the *Ubi* of God expresses itself in the commentaries on another book of poetry, the Psalms, in terms of the question of whether the *heart* or the *tongue* does the important speaking of a poem. Henry King, Canon of Christ Church in 1623 and later (1642) Bishop of Chichester, an Anglican with somewhat Puritan attitudes toward language (and himself a translator of the Psalms), writes of the Psalms that 'however betwixt *Man and Man* this verball trafficke be necessary: yet betwixt *us and God* that sees the *thoughts* before the *tongue* hath formed them into syllables; or set the stampe of language upon them, it is not so' –

So that this *Dixi* is not so much the language of *Davids* Tongue, as of his Heart; *Corde pronunciare erat*, He spake unto God in his *thoughts.*[27]

And John Hayward, whose sympathies on this matter are clearly similar to King's, says in his *Davids Teares* that 'Hee who often regardeth not the voice of the tongue, will alwayes heare the voice of our teares. The voice of the tongue is framed in the mouth, but the voice of teares proceeds from a heart, surprised either with joy or with griefe.'[28] Donne, on the other hand, admitting that God hears 'those tears, which we *cannot utter; Ineloquacibus*, as Tertullian reads that place,'[29] will not go so far as to say that the '*Ineloquacibus*' is the only voice God hears. And so, too, Herbert's poetry demonstrates the Anglican compromise, *joining* both heart and tongue. Sometimes Herbert seems to put more stock in the 'few words' truly said in 'A True Hymne' than in poetry itself, but he writes a poem about it: 'My *heart* was meaning all the day, / Somewhat it fain would say.' As in 'Longing,' the language of the heart expresses itself finally as the language of the tongue: 'Lord JESU, heare my heart, / Which hath been broken now so long, / That ev'ry part / Hath got a tongue!'

IV THE MIRROR OF THE TRINITY: HEART, MOUTH, HANDS

Herbert's 'Trinitie Sunday' extends the Augustinian idea that the Triune God (Father, Son, Holy Ghost) is mirrored in the faculties of man's soul (memory, understanding, will) to another mirror: the heart, the mouth, the hands of the poet.[30] '*Enrich my heart, mouth, hands in me*' Herbert prays at the end of his poem celebrating the unique 'three persons, one substance' nature of his God,

'With faith, with hope, with charitie; / That I may runne, rise, rest with thee.' The God 'who has form'd me out of mud' (Father), 'redeem'd me through thy bloud' (Son), 'And sanctifi'd me to do good' (Holy Ghost) expresses himself as the three-part harmony of motion (runne, rise, rest) in the writing of a poem. Proceeding from the heart (*Principium*, as the Father), the operations of the mouth (*Logos*) and the hand (making known the actions of the heart and the mouth) are *one with* the operations of the heart. To rank or separate the three vectors at work in the creation of a poem is to be guilty of a micro-form of Arianism.[31] To deny the goodness of the part of the flesh of pen and ink is to be guilty of a micro-form of gnosticism. The 'hand' of the poet *entails* both mouth and heart.[32]

The central tenet of the doctrine of the Trinity, of course, is that the notion of the Triune God explains the notion of Being to beings, God's transcendence to his immanence.[33] Primordial being (the Father) is one with expressive being (the Son) and unitive being (the Holy Ghost); it is the function of unitive being (the Holy Ghost) to repair the division between rebellious beings and their Creator (whose essence is Being). The hand of the poet, engaged in writing a poem, reflects the operations of unitive being: it repairs the great wound separating creatures from their health in Being. In a pithy Latin poem, 'On Luke the Doctor,' Herbert identifies the act of inscribing with the duty of a physician:[34] 'Why did God a *doctor* pick, / That he, filled up *with the Holy Spirit*, / Might with his consecrated hand / Record the acts of Christ?' – 'It was in order that each man / Might learn what's good for him.' The healing hand which writes (uniting beings with Being) is an emblem of reconciling love (the 'charitie' of 'Trinitie Sunday'), and its symbolism remains one of Herbert's chief arguments for the retention of religious ceremony: 'Does not the right hand even, / *The emblem of healing love*, / Escape you?' he asks the Melvillian Puritans.

Others before Herbert had explicated the 'hand which holds the pen' as a 'shadow of the Trinity':[35] 'that which the virtue of the Holy Trinity utters is written by a trinity of fingers,'[36] Cassiodorus comments. In his *Chirologia: or the Naturall Language of the Hand*, John Bulwer claims that the hand escaped the curse of Babel, that it is 'an universall character of Reason,' and that it represents 'the signifying faculties of the soule.'[37] Donne calls the hand 'The Organ of the Law, *which exalted, and rectified* Nature' (The 'Organ of Nature was the eye,' he argues).[38] But in a sermon based on Psalm 105:26 ('Then he sent Moses his servant, and Aaron whom he had chosen'), it is Lancelot Andrewes who comes closest to anticipating Herbert's own particular identification of the hand as dispenser of the Spirit and the emblem of the priesthood. Having called the ministers of God 'the hands of God,' Andrewes continues,

Out of which term, of 'the hands of God,' the people first are taught their duty, so to esteem of them, *as of God's own hands*; that as God ruleth them 'by the hands of Moses and Aaron,' that is, by their ministry, so Moses and Aaron rule them by the hands of God, that is, by His authority.[39]

Here the language of Andrewes ('as God ruleth ... hands ... so Moses and Aaron rule ... hands') reveals that he thinks of the 'hand' in terms of an analogy of proper proportion, uniting beings with Being in the hands of God: '*Heavenly and divine had those hands need be*, which are to be the hands and the work of God,' Andrewes remarks, bringing home his equation (hands = Hands). Thus, to Andrewes, the hand represents the unitive Being of the Spirit, healing and reintegrating the universe, linking beings with their Being. The 'extent' of the sacerdotal hand, as Andrewes describes it, reaching from things human to things divine, resembles well the 'extent' of the reintegrating hand of the poet-priest of *The Temple*: '*With th'one hand touching heav'n, with th'other earth*' ('Mans Medley').

As I have suggested, genuine metaphysical analogy does indeed exist in the poetry of George Herbert, but, as his poetry demonstrates, he sees analogy more properly classified as a form of equivocation:[40] 'hand' and 'Hand,' for instance, have *the name only in common*. It is the poet, the custodian of names, who alone has power to *make one*, by the action of his hand (on the surface of language), of otherwise disintegrating human experience, to make it whole in the *I AM* of God. Rarely do we find in the poetry of Herbert the complete conflation of 'hands' and 'Hands' that we find in the Aaron-Moses sermon of Bishop Andrewes ('Heavenly and divine had those hands need be'), but we find something close to it. '*There hands convey him, who conveys their hands*,' Herbert observes in 'The Priesthood,' retaining some of the distinction between the 'hands' of God's ministers and of God. It is, after all, through the sacrifice of Christ rather than through the effort of philosophy that beings find access again to their God: 'As Sampson bore the doores away,' Herbert calculates of the otherwise unspeakable distance in 'Sunday,' '*Christs hands, though nail'd, wrought our salvation, / And did unhinge that day.*' The language of the poetry of George Herbert never lets us forget the *price* of the reconciliation between man and his God, the *mysterium* of two become one. As he writes, the poet-priest '*fils up that which is behinde of the afflictions of Christ in his flesh, for his Bodie's sake, which is the Church*'

('Wherein is contained the complete definition of a Minister'): 'Be to me rather sharp and TART,' Herbert pleads in 'Paradise,' 'Then let me want *thy hand & ART.*'

Poetry, the liturgical celebration of the 'hand & ART' which is of *both* man and God, for Herbert is the touchstone ('touch': equivocally, physical and philosophical) which unites the universe with the Being of God: 'where before thou didst call on me,' Herbert muses in 'Justice (II),' 'Now I still *touch* / And harp on thee.' The hand of the poet traverses the symbolic reach of the universe in its scribal endeavour with the surface of language, for it is there, on that surface, that beings join with their Being equivocally. Herbert's address to 'Providence' ('shall I write, / And not of thee, *through whom my fingers bend / To hold my quill?*') calls attention to the gracious tenuousness with which two become one in the equivocal event of the transcription of the poem: 'the *hand* you stretch, / Is *mine* to write, as it is *yours* to raise.' The unitive 'hand' of the Spirit, at once writing in man and nailed to the Cross in God, raises creation to its own Being by lovingly communicating its own nature and poetically lending its own '*Name*' to the 'hand' which celebrates the poem. In his lover's 'Complaint' at the beginning of 'The Church' ('Love I'), Herbert remarks bitterly, 'Onely a scarf or glove / Doth *warm our hands*, and make them write of love' although 'thy glorious *name* / Wrought our deliverance from th'infernal pit.' God's one-sided love affair with man but asks for the use of man's hands, both to receive God's self-communicating 'mine' as 'thine' as in 'Clasping of hands' and to recognize 'That all things are more ours by being his' as in 'The Holdfast.' Man's spiritual-artistic history, as chronicled in *The Temple*, is told by the gradual transformation of 'cold hands,' still 'angrie with the fire' in 'Church-lock and key,' into hands which 'Strive' and 'love the strife' in the union-communion of poetry with Being in 'The Banquet': 'Let the wonder of his pitie / Be my dittie, / And *take up my lines and life*: / Hearken under pain of death, / *Hands and breath.*'

Certainly a large part of the amazing accomplishment of the poetry of George Herbert is that the poetry does not leave the paradox of *one equals two* as a phenomenon relevant to language alone. Herbert's 'Providence,' relating the logic of synonym to the logic of homonym (oneness in *things* to oneness in *words*), completes the final task of the unitive Being of the Spirit. 'All things that *are*,' Herbert concludes in 'Providence,' 'though they have sev'rall wayes, / Yet in their *being* joyn with *one* advise / To honour thee.' Privatively 'light' is made one with 'glasse' ('Light without winde is glasse'): 'light' and 'glass' are predicated synonymously – made to share the same definition. In the lengthy univocal predication of 'Providence,' the tenacious category of substance-essence ('All substance appears individual,' Aristotle comments, 'What each denotes is a unit') is broken down, fractured, into the many which reveals the one-Being, the one substance-essence of God.[41] As 'All things that are' join with '*one* advise,' so '*Each* thing that is' ('although in use and name / It *go for one*') has '*many* wayes' to honour God. Synonym is simply the obverse of homonym, reinforcing the logic of the two-one / one-two Being of God.

Writing is the predication of God to George Herbert. Praise does not just record the providence of God: praise *effects* ontology and *is itself* the providence of God continuing as creative presence in the universe. Providence is '*Gods hand in all things*' ('The Parson's Consideration of Providence'), 'a threefold power in every thing that concernes man.' As by his 'sustaining power' God 'preserves and actuates everything in his being,' so by his 'governing power' he preserves and orders the references of things one to the other, and by his 'spiritual power' he 'turnes all outward blessings to inward advantages.' Functioning as the instrument of God's threefold power, the poet (the 'worlds high Priest' and the 'Secretarie of thy praise') radiates the 'actuating' power of the Father by logically outlining the 'references of things one to the other' in the healing-reintegrating power of the Son, thereby turning all to the 'inward advantage' of the Holy Ghost. 'Providence' tells the story of that threefold power emanating from the poet: 'He that to praise and laud thee doth refrain, / Doth not refrain unto himself alone, / But robs a thousand who would praise thee fain.' Univocation is the art of the Father in the universe of *things*, equivocation is the art of the Son in the universe of *words*, and the relation between univocation and equivocation, joining *things and words* to the Being of God, is the art of the Spirit returning all (*things and/as words*) as rent to be paid back to God: 'None can express thy works, but he that knows them: / And none can know thy works ... / ... but onely he that *owes* them.'

2

The Sacramental Voice: Distance Related

I THE GARMENT OF POETIC VOICE

Through the limited, mortal, and even quite individual voice of the poet, the voice of Christ expresses itself. 'Almightie God doth grieve, *he puts on sense*,' Herbert observes in 'Ephes. 4:30' of what happens in the sacramental persona of his poem: 'I sinne not to my grief alone, / But to my Gods too; *he doth grone.*'[1] In the isolated, stilling, moments of the emotional life of one member who at times speaks as 'The Church,' the voice of Christ reveals itself, expresses itself as still suffering in his Body, which is 'The Church':

> My heart did heave, and there came forth, *O God!*
> By that I knew that *thou wast in the grief,*
> To guide and govern it to my relief.

Artistic persona for Herbert is the meeting point between his God and him: it is a garment to be *put on*. It signifies at once both Christ's putting on of humanity and humanity's putting on of Christ. 'Thy life on earth was grief,' Herbert continues, analysing the method of God's self-disclosure in 'Affliction (III)': 'and thou art still / Constant unto it, making it to be / A point of honour, *now to grieve in me, / And in thy members suffer ill.*' As poetic voice is a means for Christ to continue to express himself, so it is a means for the poet to grow into wholeness, to become *one* with Christ, in Christ and in the unity of all the members of his Body.

Like everyone else, Herbert knew all too well that human personality gives evidence of its fall from wholeness in the painful conflict of disintegrating inner voices. The fractures in the post-Adamic personality manifest themselves in 'The Church' as the poet confesses to the internal vocal opposition

between good and evil and chronicles the occasional past victories of the
Satanic over the precepted voice. '*Late when I would have something done, /
I had a motion to forbear, / Yet I went on,*' he admits in 'The Method.' In-
structive, indeed corrective, the voice of Christ frequently breaks through
the poet's eudaemonistic, self-satisfied, and self-justifying voice: Christ in-
terrupts the legal narrative of 'Love unknown' ('So I went / To fetch a sacrifice
out of my fold') with '*Your heart was hard, I fear.*' The prevailing of Christ's
voice both *is* and *will be* despite the darker triumphs of the past, despite the
history which suggests our proud division from that *One Man in Christ and
his Church*,[2] the controlling titular metaphor of Herbert's body of poems.
'The Church' is for Herbert an exercise in persona as would-be personality:
the poetry anticipates his complete participation in the personality of Christ.
'Look for *Him in me*,' Herbert urges at the end of his Latin poem 'On the
harmony of the world with Christ.' The mystery of *Him in me*, experienced
occasionally, ceremoniously, sacramentally in 'The Church,' prefigures the
total participation and wholeness of eschatological personality.

'*They part my garments*, and by lot dispose / *My coat, the type of love.*' Of
the many events surrounding Christ's passion in 'The Sacrifice,' it is this one
incident of the parting of Christ's garment which is to remain of utmost significance to the poet, *qua* poet. For the coat, the robe, the garment of Christ
is in Herbert's poetry a metaphor for the poet's voice which a man *puts on* in
speaking to God. The 'garment of style' is, of course, a concept familiar
enough to discussions of Renaissance poetics, but the garment of Herbert's
style, the texture of his poetic voice, has its origins in a country quite distant
from Renaissance rhetoric and poetic books; its weave is sacramental. 'Let us
therefore put on Jesus Christ,' John Jewell exhorts in a sermon on Romans
13:12,

Let us cover us under his apparell, as *Jacob* himselfe under the coat of his Brother *Esau*,
and so let us present our selves before our heavenly father. The phrase of putting on is
usuall: whereby he meaneth, we must be wholly clad, and possessed with Christ.[3]

His apparel, as Jewell calls it, is his voice, as Herbert practises it in his poetry.
'*A type of love*,' the garment of voice signifies the self-communicating nature
of God who puts on a voice, 'puts on sense,' by speaking as man in order that
man might speak as him. Converse with God is not speaking *to* but *in* him.

As Herbert recognizes in the first of the sonnets to his mother, 'Doth
Poetry / Wear *Venus* Livery?,' poetic voice is spun from the stuff of human
love, of man's need to communicate himself to others. By its very nature,
poetry makes conspicuous man's mortality: it calls attention to his in-

sufficiency and the sufferings which are incumbent on his body. Such a body Christ assumes in the continuance of his suffering in 'The Church.' 'Arise, arise; / And with his *buriall-linen* drie thine eyes,' Herbert solaces his heart in 'The Dawning':

> Christ left his *grave-clothes*, that we might, when grief
> Draws tears, or bloud, not want a *handkerchief*.

A metaphor for the voice of poetry itself, the 'buriall-linen' (an emblem of Christ's assumed mortality) is the equipment of prayer by which man and God meet: '*Heaven in ordinarie, man well drest.*' As 'Josephs Coat,' the torn and blood-stained garment of another son, poetic voice is 'giv'n to anguish.' It *will be* what it cannot be now – 'One of JOYES coats': 'I live to shew his power, who once did bring / My *joyes* to *weep*, and now my *griefs* to *sing.*'

In essence poetry tells the story of man's fall into sin, the story of his pulling away and alienation from God in an attempt to express *self*. Language, like the silk spun from a caterpillar making its own cocoon, is evidence of man's original solipsism: 'Now foolish thought go on, / Spin out thy thread, *and make thereof a coat / To hide thy shame*' ('Assurance'). But the original shameful clothing of poetic voice (still indulged in by the 'foolish lovers' of 'The Forerunners' who 'With canvas, not with arras, *clothe their shame*') is transfigured as 'The Church' *clothed with the Son* (Revelation 12:1). For what begins in 'Assurance' as expression of self is transformed as love and the relinquishing of the masking disguises of self in the illuminating personality and expression of the Son-Sun: 'What for it *self love* once began, / Now *love and truth* will end in man.' Poetic voice in 'The Church' renews the 'crossing' of man: it is the scarlet robe of 'The Sacrifice' which shows his blood 'to be the onely way / And cordiall left to repair mans decay.'

Unlike the conversation between man and man, where man speaks *to* man, the conversation between man and God distinguishes itself by the fact that in that language a man speaks *in* God: the roles of the addressing and the ad- dressed break down. As Michael Jermin remarks in his 1638 *Paraphrasti- cal Meditations* on the book of Proverbs, 'the eares of the Lord are in their prayers: so neere is hee to the righteous, *that his eares are joyned to their prayers, that his eares are in them.*'[4] Not trans-action, but sacramental inter- action, poetic voice in 'The Church' renews the mystery of the Cross, for God's 'hearing' by 'being in' man's dialogue-soliloquy is predicated by his blood: 'Yet heare, O God, onely for his blouds sake / Which pleads for me.' The incessant 'calling' of 'The Church' ('Lord, I fall, / Yet call') becomes an ontological establishment of its own re-calling, of its part in God as his restored image: 'Yet Lord *restore thine image, heare my call.*' In the language of Canaan the hearing is one with the calling, and that 'easie quick accesse' is established by Christ's willingness to communicate his own cries not *to* but *in us* on the Cross and in 'The Sacrifice': 'Thou canst no more not heare, then thou canst die.' God's hearing is *one with* and indistinguishable from the verse which asks to be heard: 'When my devotions could not pierce / *Thy silent eares*; / Then was my heart broken, *as was my verse.*'

By some in Reformation England an understanding of sacramentality and of the relation between Christ and his Church is referred to the tribunal of logic, by others to the terms of rhetoric itself. 'All tropes are emphaticall,' writes the interesting Puritan thinker, William Perkins, in his 'The Art of Prophesying': 'and besides delight and ornament, they affoard matter for the nourishment of faith: as when *Christ* is put for the *Christian man*, or for the *Church of God.*'⁵ Two tropes Perkins particularly identifies with the Christian mystery of *God made man*: *Anthropo-pathia*, 'whereby those things that are properly spoken of a man, are by similitude attributed to God ... His eares are put for his accepting of mens prayers,' and *sacramental Metonymy*, 'whereby the name of the adjunct, as also of the helping cause is put for the thing represented in the Sacrament: or, wherby the signe is put for the thing signified contrarily.' Language itself is a trope, both anthropo-pathetic and metonymical, in 'The Church.' God has no 'eares' with which to hear or not hear; God's 'ear' both in Herbert's poetry and in its model in the Psalms – 'I have called upon thee, O God, for thou shalt hear me: incline thine ear to me, and hearken unto my words' (Psalm 17:6) – is 'put on' anthropo-pathetically by the language which addresses him, and the language itself either prophesies (as do the Psalms) or remembers (as does Herbert's poetry) the historical event of the Incarnation. Anthropo-pathia is a metaphor of projection which allows the poet to discover within the 'accommodated' actions of God the spiritual condition of self. 'And should Gods eare, / Which needs not man, be ty'd to those / Who heare not him, but quickly heare / His utter foes?' the speaker asks in 'The Method.' Metonymy, on the other hand, another sacred trope found at the centre of the idea of language in 'The Church,' allows the poet to discover something about God: the sign (language itself) leads episte-mologically *up* the ladder of being. Looked at metonymically, the ultimate metaphor, which is the poet's 'speaking'-'crying'-'calling' in order to be 'heard' in God, does not revert back to his own humanity but directs itself anagogically to the opening of the sealed significance of all things in the last judgment ('answering') of God: 'Yet when the houre of thy designe / To *answer* these fine things shall come; / Speak not at large; say I am thine: / And they shall have their answer home.'

II THE DAVIDIC ANALOGUE

As long as he is on earth and in time, no man can be totally *in Christ*, no matter how much he may try or desire to be so. 'The Church' provides for Herbert a context in which to find and explore his greater-than-individual personality as a member of the Body of Christ, but that personality cannot be fully realized until the end of time. Appropriately, persona in 'The Church' identifies itself more directly with the prophetic personality of David as type of Christ in the Psalms than with the clarified personality of the Gospels. Encumbered and pinioned by sin, the personality which speaks in 'The Church' participates sacramentally in the voice of Christ, prophesying its own eschatological participation in Christ and all the members of his Body at the end of time. When he is heard now, Christ speaks in his Church *directively* (as *Head* of his Body and *shepherd* of his flock), leading its members to the loving-sharing-communicating participation in one another and the wholeness which pre-figures the eventual apocalyptic unity outside of time. Doctrinal statements that we are *one man in Christ* can be found, of course, throughout the New Testament. But the Psalms of the Old Testament *represent* the voice of that *one man* poetically, suffering in all the members of his Body (as Christian exegetes noted without exception), and the Psalms generically recognize themselves as prophecy.

Augustine's *Commentary on the Psalms* provided seventeenth-century religious poets with a moving, eloquent, and extended statement about the relationship between the voice of the Psalmist and the *Corpus Christi*, the Body of Christ still crying in the eternal-present of 'The Sacrifice' and continued in the temporal existence of 'The Church.' The speaker of the Psalms, Augustine argues, is a Man 'extended throughout the whole world, of which *the Head is above, the limbs below*': 'We need not then dwell long on pointing out to you, who is the speaker here: let each one of us be a member of Christ's Body; and he will be the speaker here.'[6] Persona in Herbert's 'The Church' is similarly expansive, and it invites its reader to sacramental participa-tion in its voice: 'approach, and taste / The churches mysticall repast.' Against the backdrop of Christian history's total experience recorded in Scripture, Herbert finds his own identity: 'I did towards Canaan draw; but now I am / Brought back to the Red Sea, the sea of shame.' Both poet and reader are asked to unite themselves with the re-integrating experience of 'The Church': 'So now each Christian hath his journeys spann'd.'

For Herbert all 'I's' become one 'I' in 'The Church' as each individual speaker contributes his identity to membership in Christ's Body, or 'The Church.' Like Aaron, the speaker who transcends individuality in the totality of 'The Church' discards his *old clothing* and becomes *newly dressed* in Christ's voice: 'Christ is my onely head, / My alone onely heart and breast.' Christ does not cease speaking in 'The Sacrifice.' As the speaker reminds himself in 'The Discharge': 'God did make / Thy businesse his, and *in thy life partake.*' Whether Head speaks or whether members speak, Augustine argues in his commentary on Psalm 75, Christ speaks: 'He speaketh in the person of the Head, He speaketh in the person of the Body.'[7] '*This is a great Sacrament,*' Augustine continues (interpreting the Psalms through St Paul), '*I,* he saith, *speak in Christ and in the Church* ... let us hear Him, and in Him let us also speak.'

What Augustine's *Commentary on the Psalms* does (and what neither the Psalms nor the Gospels do in themselves) is to read the Davidic prophecy of Christ's sufferings on the Cross as spoken *in his own person and in ours.* This makes 'The Sacrifice,' of course, crucial to all that follows in 'The Church,' for the voice of the Church is predicated on the final moments of Christ's mortal nature when he hung *forsaken* of his Father ('But, *O my God, my God!* why leav'st thou me'). Psalm 22, which prophesies the humiliation (at times in gruesome detail – 'For many dogs are come about me') and the theology ('I am poured out like water') of the Crucifixion, and even the parting of the garments ('They part my garments among them, and cast lots upon my vesture'), finds many verbal echoes in 'The Sacrifice.' But it is the concept of 'the *words* of my complaint' (Psalm 22:1) and, particularly, of a God 'so *far from my health* and *from the words of my complaint*' that most deeply influences Augustine's interpretation of the entire Psalm and, through it, Herbert's 'The Sacrifice.' At the head of the Psalm, Augustine argues, are *the words which sustain also the person of the old man*: 'For *our old man was nailed together with Him* to the Cross.'[8] The final words, history in the Gospel and prophecy in Psalm 22:1 ('My God, my God, look upon me; why has thou forsaken me?'), are '*The words of my sins,*' according to Augustine: 'For it is the old man nailed to the Cross that speaks, ignorant even of the reason why God hath forsaken him.'[9] The final cry is a trope, given for us, Augustine explains: 'He uttered from the Cross not His own cry, but ours.'[10] Explicating not the historical event in the Gospels but the *literary* event (prophesying history) in the Psalms, Augustine describes Christ as '"transferring us in a figure" to what He was saying, and to His own Body.'[11] The same trope of *our old man transferred in a figure* heads 'The Church' in 'The Sacrifice': 'Lo, here I hang, charg'd with a world of sinne,' Christ observes. Christ's request, 'Onely let others say, when I am dead, / Never was grief like mine,' is answered in 'The Thanksgiving' of 'The Church': 'Was such a grief as cannot be.'

As prophecy (and, therefore, imperfect history) the Psalms do not reveal the voice of the hypostatically unified personality of Christ but the voice of his mortality, as Augustine's *Commentary* insists: 'Because then He was of the seed of David, not after His Godhead, whereby He is the Creator of David, but after the flesh ... hear the voice of His Body.'[12] Words, in the Psalmist's *literary* prefiguration of the *history* on the Cross, are the basis of the economy of the Cross and its first 'law' of 'transferred' accounts. As Christ transfers us 'in a figure' to what he is saying on the Cross, Augustine maintains, he 'transfigures' us into himself: 'He who disdained not to assume us unto Himself, did not disdain to transfigure us into Himself, and to *speak with our words*, that *we too might speak with his words*.'[13] The SACRIFICE, then, becomes 'mine' ('O let thy blessed SACRIFICE be mine') as 'The Altar' promises, giving 'The Church' its proper idiom of speaking not *to* but *in* and *as* the suffering God. The 'foure words, my words, *Thy will be done*' which conclude Herbert's poem entitled 'The Crosse' are at once both 'my' and 'thy' words, words which 're-sign' Gethsemane's transfiguration of human into divine will: 'nevertheless, *not as I will but as thou wilt*' (Matthew 26:39, Mark 14:36). The equivocal sign, pointing at once to poet and to Christ, is once '*felt*' unequivocally, 'properly,' as the Cross. The terms of the equivocation in the 'figure' (the sign) spell distance enough, as in 'The Agonie': 'Love is that liquor sweet and most divine, / *Which my God feels as bloud; but I, as wine*.' And it is the business of poetry to 'measure' the distance between the human ('*O let this cup passe*') and divine ('*Thy will be done*') in the reconciling 'sameness' of a word, or 'foure words.' Explicating the price of the elements in the sign of the transformed will, Christ expounds on his own text in 'The Sacrifice': 'and my hearts deare treasure / Drops bloud (the onely beads) *my words to measure*.'

'No scrue, no piercer can / Into a piece of timber work and winde, / As Gods afflictions into man,' Herbert concedes in 'Confession.' The equivocation of the Cross (when Christ spoke *our words as his words*) made it impossible to escape his presence in our words as that agonizing grief, spanning us through the vast distance between the terms of the equivocation (human and divine), in the continuing history of 'The Church.' The drama of the relationship between the individual (limited in his notion of 'self') and 'The Church' centres on his struggle to recognize his own voice for what it is, the voice of 'The Church.' Of course, this is a privilege which David, as prophet of the voice of the Church, never enjoyed; but in 'The Church' prophecy momentarily intersects with history when the speaker acknowledges, *confesses*, his part in Christ. Ironically, the 'open breast' of 'Confession' 'shuts out' the persistent afflictions of God by attributing them to God: 'Smooth open hearts no fastning have.' It is what Herbert calls the 'fiction,' the *fiction* of individual expression and poetic invention ('Who sayes that *fictions* onely and false hair / Become a verse') which allows affliction to take hold: 'but *fiction* / Doth give a hold and handle to affliction.'

The 'fiction' of individual experience and its dispersion by the event and *fact* of sacred history is the story that Herbert's five 'Affliction' poems tell as the speaker progresses from the distancing complaint of 'Affliction (i)' ('But with my yeares sorrow did twist and grow') to the acceptance in 'Affliction (v)' of his condition *in* the Body of Christ (not as 'I' but 'we'): 'Affliction then is *ours*.' Betrayed to a 'lingring book' in 'Affliction (i),' the speaker maintains an 'Academick' stance which renders him a poor interpreter: 'what thou wilt do with me / *None of my books will show*.' As a reader of Biblical text ('I reade, and sigh, and wish I were a tree'), the speaker dramatizes himself as one still innocent about its method (wherein history is prophecy and prophecy is history), for he must still learn that Biblical interpretation *is* fulfilment, that *he is the tree* ('a tree planted by the water-side, that bringeth forth his fruit in due season' – Psalm 1:3). 'Affliction (ii),' which marks his intellectual awakening to the ontology of exegesis itself and the idea that he is the text ('Thy crosse took up in one, / By way of imprest, all my future mone'), prepares the speaker for the full disclosure of 'Affliction (iii)' that he and his God are *both* the text: 'Thy life on earth was grief, and thou art still / Constant unto it.' As he begins 'Affliction (v),' the speaker presents himself as a fully educated reader who understands the historico-prophetical dynamics of his text: 'My God, I *read* this day, / That planted Paradise was not so firm, / As *was and is* thy floting Ark.'

Until it recognizes itself as spokesman for what 'was and is,' the voice which is heard in 'The Church' plays itself off against the Psalms in ironic echoes which identify it more with the awaiting type (David) than with that which it awaits and is (the Church). Proper understanding brings the voice from the incomplete shadows of imperfect knowledge ('Thou art my grief alone, / Thou Lord *conceal* it not') to epistemologically revealed history ('*Now* thou wouldst taste our miserie'). 'Kill me not ev'ry day,' the speaker requests in 'Affliction (ii),' echoing the 'all the day long do I call upon thee' of the Psalms (86:3). Here, early in his interpretive career, the speaker *distinguishes* his own afflictions from those of his Lord: 'Thy one death for me / Is more then all my deaths can be.' The speaker has not yet, if you will, acquired the exegetical skills of St Augustine, who understood the imperative prayer of the Psalmist as an indicative trope: 'from the time that the body of

Christ groans being in afflictions, until the end of the world, when afflictions pass away, that man groaneth and calleth upon God: and each one of us after his measure hath his part in the cry of the whole body.'[14]

III SACRAMENTUM AND REM SACRAMENTI

Although the manner of the 'presence' in the Blessed Sacrament is the most highly disputed article of faith in the Church of seventeenth-century England, there is a consensus of opinion on one point: that in the Sacrament, as Irenaeus had maintained (Book IV, c. 34), there is an *earthly* and a *heavenly* part.[15] 'The body then which we eat, is in heaven: above all Angels, and Archangels ... Our met is in *heaven* on high, and we are here below on the *earth*,' John Jewell states in 1570.[16] In a sermon delivered before Commons in February, 1620, James Ussher argues more elaborately but similarly, 'If any doe further inquire, how it is possible that any such union should be, seeing the body of Christ is in *heaven*, and wee are upon *earth*': 'we should suppose a body be as high as the heavens, that the head thereof should be where Christ our Head is, and the feet where we his members are ... the same soul that is in the head, as in the fountaine of sense and motion, is present likewise in the lowest member of the body.'[17] Turning the Irenaeus commonplace into an argument against the Roman doctrine of Transubstantiation, John Cosin writes in a letter to Richard Montagu in 1630, 'So that here wee have a most manifest declaration of the Catholick faith and doctrine in these elder ages of the Church; that in the Blessed Sacrament, there is a *terrene*, and a *celestial* part, consisting (even after it is consecrate by invocation) of the earthly substance of bread, and the heavenly substance of Christ's Body, and not that one is transubstantiated into the other.'[18] As late as 1662, the Bishop of Gloucester, William Nicolson, still turns to the Irenaeus *res terrena & coelestis* trope: 'It was long since said by *Irenaeus*, that the Eucharist did consist of two parts, the one *earthly*, the other *heavenly*: to which all posterity hath assented, with one voice testifying that in the Sacrament there be Signs and Things.'[19] All this corresponds quite exactly to the idea of the relation between heaven and earth which one encounters in Herbert's poem entitled 'The H. Communion' ('Thou hast restor'd us to this ease / By this thy *heav'nly* bloud; / Which I can go to, when I please, / And leave *th'earth* to their food') and in the poems surrounding it: in 'Faith' ('I can walk to *heav'n* well neare'), in 'Prayer (I)' ('The Christian plummet sounding *heav'n and earth*'), in 'Antiphon (I)' ('The *heav'ns* are not too high, / ... The *earth* is not too low'), and, finally, in 'The Temper (I)':

Whether I *flie with angels, fall with dust*,
  Thy hands made both, and I am there:
  Thy power and love, my love and trust
    Make one place ev'ry where.

'What learne you of this?' James Ussher asks catechistically of sacramental doctrine in his *Of Christian Religion*, eliciting the answer: 'Not to stick to the outward elements, but to lift up our hearts unto God, *accounting the elements as a Ladder* whereby to climb up to those celestial things which they represent.'[20] In a 1638 sermon entitled *Immanuel, or the Mystery of the Incarnation of the Son of God* Ussher explicates that typological ladder further: 'Jacob in his dreame beheld *a ladder set upon the earth* ... Whence we may well collect, that the onely meanes whereby God standing above, and his Israel lying here below are conjoyned together, and *the onely ladder whereby Heaven may be scaled by us*, is the *Son of man*.'[21] Such *scaling of the ladder* between heaven and earth, at once sacramental and incarnational, is a major activity in *The Temple* as the poet is racked through the distances ('O rack me not to such a vast extent') that the sacramentality of his language implies. In his section on the Sacrament in *The Country Parson*, Herbert explains, 'for thou art not only the feast, but *the way to it*.' It is the *way*, together with its excruciating ups and downs, which is the story that 'The Church' tells: 'let thy gracious power / Contract my houre, / *That I may climbe and finde relief*,' the poet begs in 'Complaining.' To journey forth from the land of Egypt (this world) to the land of Canaan (in the Father) is the intention of the poetry and the aim of its language. The vertical journey imagery throughout the volume of poems tells the story of the poet's spiritual-artistic progress towards a complete understanding of his medium.

As Herbert tells us in 'The Flower,' these are God's wonders: 'Killing and quickening, bringing down to *hell* / And up to *heaven* in an houre' –

  But while I grow in a straight line,
Still upwards bent, *as if heav'n were mine own*,
  Thy anger comes, and I decline.

'Mans medley' joins his 'terrene' and the 'celestial' parts as the singer scales the ladder Immanuel (*God with us*): 'Man ties them both alone, / *And makes them one*.' But the sacramental *making one*, the poet's equivocal task in joining the Head (above) and the Body (below), is a noble purpose not without its tensions. And the poet's 'story' reveals the agony and the strain of speaking the language of Canaan. 'What have I left, that I should stay and grone,' Herbert asks in 'Home,' when *'most of me to heav'n is fled'*: 'And *ev'n my verse*, when by the ryme and reason / The word is, *Stay*, sayes ever, *Come.'* Here, in the sign, on the surface of the poem itself, one finds the vast 'extent' of the sacramentality of Herbert's language, passing forth from the bondage that *is* here below to the land of Canaan in heaven above as a word discloses its own antonym in its struggle against its natural slavery to description of the empirical world: *'Stay'-'Come.'*

Joining heaven and earth, Head and Body, in sacramental moments of communion which relieve the strain of its dimensions (*making one place everywhere*), language in 'The Church' enjoys the logical function understood by seventeenth-century Anglicanism to be operative in the Sacrament. In his 1620 House of Commons sermon Ussher explains the twofold nature of the Sacrament by employing the logical notion of 'Relation':

a Sacrament taken in his full extent, comprehendeth two things in it: that which is outward and visible, which the Schooles call properly *Sacramentum*, (in a more strict acception of the word;) and that which is inward and invisible, which they tearme *rem Sacramenti* the principall thing exhibited in the Sacrament ... in the outward part of this mysticall action, which reacheth to that which is *Sacramentum* onely, we receive this body and blood but sacramentally; in the inward, which containeth *rem*, the thing it selfe in it, wee receive them really: and consequently the presence of these in the one is *relative and symbolicall*; in the other, *reall and substantiall.*[22]

Considerably later, in the 1660s, William Nicolson still holds fast to the logical notion of Relation in his definition of the Sacrament ('The form of the Sacrament consists in Relation, which is the mutuall respect betwixt the sign and the things signified, such as is between the father and his son'), using it on the one hand to dismiss the Roman doctrine of transubstantiation (the *suppositum Relati* is not turned into the *suppositum Correlati*: 'the *signum* and the *signatum* would be all one, which overthrows the definition'), and using it on the other, to present and maintain a precise definition of the *real presence*: 'Really, puts us in mind of the last end, to Seal: and such a reall presence must be admitted, or else the Communicant receives nothing.'[23] Cosin too had been eager to demonstrate the logical inconsistency of the doctrine of transubstantiation, what Nicolson calls the 'chimera of Thomas's brain': 'As the two Natures in Christ, so the signe, (Bread and Wine) and the thing signified in the Sacrament, (the Body and Bloud of Christ) are neither of them annulled, or transubstantiated one into another.'[24] But it is the more elaborate examination of the *two as one* trope set forth by John Wilcoks which

resembles most Herbert's both-one, one-both demonstration of the sacramentality of equivocacy (*one* word-sign meaning *both*) in *The Temple*: 'the
outward and visible signe,' Wilcoks argues, is 'in effect but one, though in
number two ... formally the signes and the things signed, are but one, but
materially two, saith the School.'[25]

Ontology does not break down in seventeenth-century Anglican Eucharistic doctrine but becomes more intricately argued as its Thomistic analogical
structure is replaced by the notion of logical Relation. Heaven meets with
earth, earth reaches into heaven, and that ontological passage is recorded in
the poetry of Herbert. The 'outward signe' and the 'inward grace' (*'Rem
terrenam & Caelestem'*), Wilcoks insists, *become one in the Communion*: 'we
come now to the Communion, or their *coming into one*, to make up the
Sacrament: though the one part be on earth, the other in heaven; and look
how high the heaven is from earth, yet they may meet, *they must meet, else
there will be no Sacrament at all.*'[26] Ontological continuity, sustained by the
great chain of being in Thomistic analogy, is not a given in the world as we
have it, according to much of the thinking in Herbert's time. Such integrity
once existed: 'Before that sinne turn'd flesh to stone, / And all our lump to
leaven; / A fervent sigh might well have blown / Our innocent earth to
heaven' ('The H. Communion'). Rather, the *Sacrament* restores the break in
the chain ('Thou hast *restor'd* us to this ease') by *joining* the sign to the thing
signed in the 'Union' which is 'Communion': 'Thus have we made the signes,
and the things signed to meet,' Wilcoks concludes in his important sermon.
For Herbert, as poet, 'sign' and 'thing signed' meet in equivocated language
which can restore, *as does the Sacrament*, a logical relation between earth and
the heavenly Canaan.

'Or can not leaves, but fruit, be *signe* / Of the *true vine*?' Here, in 'Good
Friday,' we encounter Herbert explicitly considering the meeting (union-
communion) of the *rem terrenam* and the *rem coelestem* in 'signe.' The
question, 'Or can not leaves, but fruit,' like the other questions in 'Good
Friday' ('How shall I measure out thy bloud' and 'Shall I thy woes / Number'), is a non-question: the poet is already 'measuring' and 'numbering' in
the 'measures' and 'numbers' of verse, and the point is that *both* leaves and
fruit are sign of the vine (Christ – 'thing signed'). The sign, language itself
('leaves' are a commonplace metaphor for 'words'),[27] is the meeting point of
the 'Relation' between the Vine (Being) and its fruit (in creatures-history-
beings): the sign restores the ontological integrity of the universe, as does the
Sacrament, in the union-communion of what Herbert calls 'Love,' and that
love manifests itself logically as *relation*. The 'original' *distance* to be overcome in the Sacrament by the sign, the distance between fruit-history and

vine-Christ-Being, is measured by the thorns of 'The Sacrifice': 'Then on my head a crown of thorns I wear: / For these are all the *grapes* Sion doth bear, / Though I my *vine* planted and watred there.' And the discrepancy measured by 'The Sacrifice' is repaired in 'The Agonie' by the ontological bridge of Communion-union-Love ('Who knows not *Love*, let him assay / And *taste that juice*') which draws together into '*Relation*' of sign-signed both wine and blood: '*Love is that liquour sweet* and most divine, / Which my God feels as *bloud*; but I, as *wine*.'

Lending us an exact vocabulary with which to discuss the dynamic vectors which operate in language which strives after sacramentality, Wilcoks further specifies the nature of the 'Relation' that obtains in the Sacrament: 'The Bloud of Christ *Metonimically*, the merit of his Bloud; that which he effected by shedding of his Bloud.'[28] Basing his statement on the rules of logic, Wilcoks explains that 'a substance cannot be a Relation, but by a *Metonymy of the effect*.'[29] Such 'Relation,' held together by 'Metonymy of the effect,' structures the poetic ellipsis of Herbert's 'The Banquet' as the speaker travels fearlessly between the *relatum* and the *correlatum* of the wine and the blood ('God took bloud, and needs would be / Spilt with me, / ... Sweetly he doth meet my taste'), for he is justified in the 'effect' of the *merit* of the blood of Christ: 'Wine becomes a wing at last. / For with it alone I flie / To the skie.' Other forms of metonymy, and indeed synecdoche (relating not just adjunctively but con-junctively), are present in the poem; in fact, the poem is *about* metonymy and its stronger form, synecdoche.[30] In 'The Banquet' we see the dynamics of sacred trope: 'tasting' is related to the 'telling' through the mutual 'adjunct' of the tongue ('Thy delight / Passeth *tongue* to *taste or tell*'). And the consecrated metaphor of artistic experience brings God ontologically down the sacramental ladder of the poem itself (God 'so found me on the ground') at the same time that it brings its speaker epistemologically up that ladder: 'Him I view.' What is more, speaker, God, and poem *become one* (as the 'musick ... three parts vied / And multiplied') in the union-communion of song itself: 'Let the wonder of his pitie / *Be my dittie*, / And take up my *lines and life*.' Symbol here, an icon joining 'life' to 'lines,' does not dissolve into human reception (the Puritan teleological 'heart'): poetry, as Herbert understands it, is the chief surgeon of the universe, mending the broken bones of the Body whose Head is above and whose limbs below: 'Lord, thy broken consort raise, / And *the musick shall be praise*.'

Maintaining that Sacraments 'relatively united unto the things which they doe signifie' are *seals* as well as *signs* ('wee acknowledge Sacraments to be *signes*; but bare *signes* we denie them to bee: *seales* they are, as well as signes of the Covenant of grace'), Bishop Ussher upholds the ontology of sacramental symbol: 'Neither are they to be accounted barely *significative*, but truly *exhibitive* also of those heavenly things whereto they have relation: as being appoynted by God to be a meanes of *conveying the same unto us, and putting us into actuall possession thereof.*'[31] Such 'sealing' (beyond mere 'signing') can be seen operating in Herbert's poem, 'The H. Communion' ('Not in rich furniture, or fine aray, / ... To me dost now *thy self convey*'). On the one hand, the speaker refuses to conflate the two elements of the Relation ('Yet can these not get over to my soul, / Leaping the wall that parts / Our souls and fleshy hearts'), and, on the other hand, he understands the doctrine of *gracious exhibition* ('Onely thy grace, which with these elements comes'); but there can be no doubt that he also assumes an effectual presence: 'as th'outworks, they may controll / My rebel-flesh, and *carrying thy name,* / Affright both sinne and shame.' A sign and the thing signified 'are so neerly conjoyned together' in the Sacrament, Ussher claims, '*that the name* of the one is usually communicated to the other.'[32] Similar (if not identical) is the dynamic of Herbert's poem, as the *name* given the 'outworking' external thing ('my Body') communicates itself to 'the souls most subtile rooms' in the delicate balance of *Relation* rather than conflation. And that communicated 'name' equivocally predicates the presence of Christ to the speaker: 'Making thy way my rest, / And thy small quantities my length.'

While explaining that in the logic of 'relation' operative in sacramental 'sign' the *name* of the one thing is communicated to the other, Ussher provides a literary, or linguistic, analogue: 'So words being the signes of things, no sooner is the sound of the word conveyed to our eares, but the notion of the thing signified thereby is presented to our minde: and thereupon in the speech of Scripture nothing is more ordinary, then by the terme of *Word* to denote a thing.'[33] The task with which Herbert as poet confronts himself is developing a system for conveying heavenly 'things' (things beyond things) to the words which match things on earth. Sacramentality ensures that system, lending heaven to words in what Ussher calls 'this relative kinde of presence.' Language itself becomes the '*shewbread*,' '*the bread of faces*,' '*the presence bread*,' of the Sacrament; and of such material is the 'face' of 'The Church' composed, exhibiting the *real presence* in its 'letters.'

IV *JAH*: BEING AND THE NAME

'How hath man parcel'd out thy glorious name, / And thrown it on the dust which thou hast made.' Herbert's complaint in 'Love (1)' tells in short form the story of the 'original' separation of beings from their Being: all things should *name* not themselves but God (in whom they *are*). 'We say amisse, /

This or that *is*.' As Herbert sees it, it is the duty of the religious poet to return all things to their proper name in praise of God: 'all wits shall rise, / And praise him who did make and mend our eies.' Poetry re-integrates language and that which it properly names, as Herbert tells us in 'Longing': 'Let not the winde / Scatter *my words, and in the same / Thy name!*' In 're-entitling' God to the world of his creatures, poetry builds a ladder between the 'scattered' name of God (the 'parcelled out' evidence of what *is* in the world of creatures) and the fountain of all Being above: 'That all things were more ours by being his.' By giving things back to God in his name ('*Roses* and *Lillies* speak thee' – 'Will not a verse run smooth that bears thy name?'), poetry gives back to the decaying world its *being* in the great *I AM* of God's name.

When we encounter Herbert invoking God's name ('Wherefore each part / Of my hard heart / Meets in this frame, / *To praise thy name*'), we do well to realize that the name is *I am that I am* and that, as most men in the seventeenth century knew full well, 'It importeth that God *Is*, & hath his being of himselfe before all worlds, *Isa. 44:6*, that he giveth *being* or existence unto all things, and in him all are and consist, *Act. 17:25*, that he giveth *being* unto his word, effecting whatsoever he hath spoken.'[34] For Augustine the name of God carries with it a singularly temporal message, that men 'may hope in those things which flow by, in time's quick revolution, having nothing but "will be" and "has been" ... in the nature of God nothing will be, as if it were not yet; or hath been, as if it were no longer: but there is only that which is.'[35] Removing things from 'will be'-'has been' into the eternity which 'is,' the name of God in Herbert's poetry operates with a similar Augustinian temporal-transfer function, as in 'Whitsunday': 'Lord, though we change, thou art the same; / ... Restore this day, *for thy great name*, / Unto his ancient and miraculous right.' Not without paradox ('thy time to come is gone'), the Pentecostal meeting of Being and its beings in 'The Discharge' reclaims the world of creatures in genitive univocacy: '*Thy life is Gods*' – '*The crop is his*' ('God did make / Thy businesse his, and in thy life partake'). As Herbert's genitive univocacy re-predicates, it re-names and baptizes creatures into the being-imparting name of God, 're-calling' them from what they were 'miscalled' in sin: 'You taught the *Book of Life my name*, that so, / Whatever future sinnes should me *miscall*, / Your first acquaintance might discredit all.' And that univocacy is made possible only by the eternal intermediary equivocacy of the Cross: 'The *crosse* taught all wood to *resound his name*, / *Who bore the same*.'

In his important catechism, *A Body of Divinitie*, Bishop Ussher sets forth the question 'Is there nothing of God to be known besides his name?,' to which his answer is, 'Nothing as touching his beeing, falling under our weak and shallow capacity.'[36] Asking, 'What names of God in the Scripture are derived from these words?,' he answers, 'Two, the name of *Jehovah*, and the name *Jah*, both which being drawn from this description of God, doth set forth his essence and beeing, teaching us that his eternall and almighty beeing (whom no creature is able to conceive) dependeth of no other cause, but standeth himself.' Then Ussher asks, 'Whence may the description of God be taken?,' in order to answer, 'From the things whereby he doth manifest himself, called in Scripture his name, *Psal. 145:1.2.3.*' Discarding the Thomistic notion of analogy as a means of coming into knowledge of God ('there can no definition be given of him; seeing every definition is an explication of the nature of the thing defined by words expressing the materiall and formal cause thereof, but of the first cause there can be no causes, therefore no words to expresse them'), Ussher and others in the seventeenth century posited the superiority of 'manifestation' over 'description' in making known the essential Being of God. And the replacement of 'definition' by 'exhibition' in the logical predication of God may well have been a major factor determining the composition of a proportionately large body of religious poetry in the seventeenth century and, more certainly, George Herbert's. Poetry takes on the job of demonstrating rather than defining the name of God who, as 'All,' contradicts the nature of a definition.

In the poem preceding 'Divinitie' with its explicit rejection of 'definitions' ('curious questions and divisions'), Herbert dramatizes the basic separation of the 'being' of definition ('this or that is') from the 'being' that is God's. 'The Method' locates Thomistic analogical predication not on the ontological ladder of being but in the realm of unrealized potential: 'Thy Father could / Quickly effect, what thou dost move; / For he is *Power*: and sure he would; / For he is *Love*.' As it is meant to, the poem falls flat; its language has no 'extent,' and the definition genre obscures rather than reveals the heaven that it grasps for (as the next poem tells us): '*Faith* needs no *staffe of flesh*, but stoutly can / To heav'n alone both go, and leade.' In the poem following 'Divinitie,' however, what had been an inactive definition two poems before becomes electric in its operation and demonstration of the *being* of God revealing himself in action: the 'God of strength and power' *grieves* for a worm, the 'God of love *doth grieve*,' and 'Almightie God *doth grieve*' and *put on sense* in 'Ephes. 4:30,' moving between the height of what he is in himself and human history where he expresses himself. In the sequence from 'The Holdfast' to 'Complaining,' the 'Mightyness' of the 'All-mightie' name of God comes to dominate the being of the poem as what the speaker considers to be his own '*power* and *might*' is relegated to the non-actual. Realizing, rather, that he '*might* trust in God' and that it is God who is that power and might (and that, properly, it is *his* name), the speaker concedes and pleads, 'Do not beguile my heart, / Because thou art / *My power and wisdome.*'

Discovering God's name in the operations of both world and poem is the major reflective act in the poetry of *The Temple*, and on this act 'The Elixir' comments: 'Teach me, my God and King, / *In all things thee to see.*' The process of re-integrating the one name which has been 'parcelled out' to the scattered dust of individuated creatures, separate in language, is a priestly act analogous to the consecration in the Sacrament: it establishes a *relation* between the apparent thing (*sacramentum*) and the real (*rem sacramenti*). 'All may of thee partake,' the speaker assures in sacramental language, 'Nothing can be so mean, / Which with this tincture (*for thy sake*) / Will not grow bright and clean.' Naming as God's, which is the responsibility of the divine poet, unveils the celestial within this terrene part and displays the heavenly in the dust of earth: 'A man that looks on glasse, / On it may stay his eye; / Or if he pleaseth, through it passe, / And then the *heav'n* espie.'

In his task of one-naming, the poet aims at manifesting what had been predicated for centuries as the 'simplicity' of God. Winding through paradox (live-die) and rhetorical involution (deserved praise-praise deserved), 'A Wreath' aspires for the structure of tautology (live-live, know-know), an equation which manifests the simplicity of God to the poet: 'Give me simplicitie, that I may live, / So live and like, that I may know, thy wayes.' Living, found only in the one and 'simple' *being* of God, transcends the variety of history and the many, 'for *life* is straight, / Straight as a line, and ever tends to thee.' The 'deceit' of the many (seeming 'above simplicitie'), demonstrating itself in the *sequence* of words in the poem's hieroglyph, is subverted by the '*line*' (the equivocal 'line' of poetry) that 'ever tends to thee.' Iconographically, the poem says what Herbert says of Christian hermeneutics in *The Country Parson* ('all truth being consonant to it self, and being penn'd by one and the self-same Spirit ... comparing place with place must be a singular help for the right understanding') and again in 'The H. Scriptures' ('Oh that I knew how all thy lights combine, / ... This verse marks that'). In 'A Wreath' language itself is 'collated' (live-live, know-know) – word is collated with word, suggesting oneness in the *res terrena* of the icon of poetry itself, a oneness which extends and equivocates to include the *res coelestis* of Canaan: 'then shall I give / For this poore wreath, give thee a crown of praise.'

Providing a parable of the artist as speller, 'Jesu' depicts the primary responsibility of the artist in reintegrating the sacred name of God. Found broken into 'parcels,' the name is unified and made whole by the activity of the poet ('I sat me down to spell them'): 'J' (I), 'U' (you), and 'ES' (is-*esse*-am) together express themselves first as '*I ease you*' (the name of the Deity man-

ifesting himself as '*I am you*') and then as 'JESU.' Multiplicity (the broken
pieces) is un-named by the poet-priest who sacrifices to the Name which is all,
discovering the consonancy in truth and transcending the Many of his Fall.
Man's original sin, understood in *The Temple* as his mis-naming and mis-
calling, is reversed by the act of the poet who re-names and re-calls into the
Name and Call of God: '*Roses* and *Lillies* speak thee.' Made possible only by
Christ's willingness to be 'parcel'd out' and 'broken' as the Many (to be shak-
en in the 'great affliction' of this world without life in his name), the re-
integration of the universe is the onus put on the divine poet, who perpetuates
the meaning of that sacrifice by the staged but humiliating discoveries of his
own misnomers: 'Or if such deceits there be, / Such delights I meant to say; /
There are no such things to me, / Who have pass'd my right away.'

'Or if I stray, he doth *convert* / And bring *my minde in frame*,' Herbert
rests assured in his own 'The 23d Psalme,' 'And all this not for my desert, /
But for his holy name.' Inverting the usual dynamics of naming (or 'calling')
by which the word points to something beyond itself, the 'holy name' is an
end in itself which does not point to some 'thing' beyond it, for it is what *is*. As
it operates in Herbert's poetry, the sacred name draws the speaker away from
the referential and individuating phenomena of the names of the Creatures
into the All of consonant Truth, the 'tender grass' and the 'gentle streams' of
God's 'worde and Sacraments.'[37] The role of the poet as pastor is to lead into
proper meaning (as the shepherd who leads his sheep to green pastures); his
role is to recall what the world miscalls. His voice is woven of the stuff of
hermeneutic intercession, mediating between the vision of God and the vision
of man by raising men's sights in the sacramental cup of the poem itself, as it
once raised his own.

In the poems at the beginning of 'The Church' there is a very marked hiatus
between the uninstructed persona of the poem, masked in the naïveté of the
Christian initiate, and the author who controls the dramatization of a speaker who does not yet know all that the author knows. As the chasm between
'voice' and 'Herbert' narrows in the development of 'The Church,' the speaker that we hear grows into oneness with the whole Body of Christ, speaking unanimously, reintegrating its fractured members, *now called one*, and
now both teaching and taught. Private complaint then grows into public
'Call' (an extended and equivocated term which identifies the poet's 'naming'
with God's 'summoning' into his Name), and that 'Call' of Herbert's poetry
both posits and celebrates the atonement between human 'voice' (committed
originally to the Many) and the divine 'Word' (which is *one* and *all*).

In Herbert's poem entitled 'The Call,' the stillness of all that God is in
himself (Way, Truth, Life; Light, Feast, Strength; Joy, Love, Heart) is made

to shatter into the fragmented progression of human history and to express itself by relating itself to something lesser: *Such a Way, as gives us breath: / Such a Truth, as ends all strife: / Such a Life, as killeth death.*' The absolute nouns which denote God abstractly (Light, Joy) descend into relation to man, into the relativity of verb and time (giving, making, mending, showing – 'Such a Light, *as shows a feast*') in order to re-call both verbs and history into that stillness of both name and noun: 'Such a Joy, as none can move: / Such a Love, as none can part: / Such a Heart, as joyes in love.' The invocative which is the call – 'Come' – is the grammatical idiom of the middle way, of the poet himself both tortured and racked between heaven and earth, eternity and history, noun and verb, absolute stillness and relative activity. Like Christ himself who *came to call*, the poet-priest-preacher of *The Temple* continues the 'calling' tradition of *kerygma*, occupying 'the space / Betwixt this world and that of grace,' and, thereby, filling up '*that which is behinde of the afflictions of Christ in his flesh, for his Bodies sake, which is the Church.*'

Language baptized (christened and re-named) into the oneness of God's name in 'The Church' (brought 'to Church well drest and clad' – 'wilt thou leave the Church?') is the 'broider'd coat' of Christ's love (once parted), repaired by the 'high Priest' in poetry. The 'cuttings' of the artist which seem to divide still further the once 'seamless coat' of language-communication-love are the 'sharpnes' which 'shows the sweetest FREND' – 'And such beginnings touch their END.' Analysis (such as the univocal-equivocal anatomy of 'Providence') unwinds the simplicity of the Deity, for it works to transcend the individuality of each thing. All things and all words, as well as the relation between things and words, are made to 'spell' God, whose name *is* (*I AM*). All becomes one equivocally; one becomes All univocally; and All is one as the priest *calls* into the union-communion of the Sacrament: 'Where is All, there All should be.'

3

Augustinianism: The Use and Enjoyment of Poetry

George Herbert gives no more succinct definition of the nature of his poetry than he does in 'The Quidditie.' In a reasonably straightforward statement, Herbert works through the *via negativa* of 'My God, a verse is not a crown, / ... nor yet a lute' to the clarity of his final positive definition: 'But it is that which *while I use / I am with thee.*' In spite of its simplicity, Herbert's direct identification of his poetry with '*use*' has gone both unannotated and un-explicated.[1] 'Some things are to be enjoyed, others to be *used*,' Augustine comments in the central passage of *De Doctrina*, 'and there are others which are to be enjoyed and used'[2] –

Those things which are to be enjoyed make us blessed. Those things which are to be *used* help and, as it were, *sustain us as we move toward blessedness* in order that we may gain and cling to those things which make us blessed.

For George Herbert poetry is to be *used* to attain those things which are to be *enjoyed*; and those things which are to be enjoyed, Augustine explains, 'are the Father, the Son, and the Holy Spirit, a single Trinity, a certain supreme thing common to all who enjoy it, if, indeed, it is a thing and not rather the cause of all things, or both a thing and a cause.'[3] Enjoyment of the things of this world as an *end* in themselves is *ab-use*, according to Augustine: 'To enjoy something is to cling to it with love for its own sake. To use something, however, is to employ it in obtaining that which you love, provided it is worthy of love. For an *illicit use* should be called rather a waste or *abuse*.'[4] Much of the story that *The Temple* tells is of the poet's struggle in adhering to the principle of poetry as use and in preventing its ab-use, which for Herbert is the enjoyment of his poetry in and for itself. Earthly enjoyment of the song shackles its singer 'by an inferior love' and retards his progress toward the real end which is the 'JOY' of 'Heaven.'

Herbert is not the only one in the seventeenth century to translate the Augustinian notion of 'use and enjoyment' (*uti-frui*) to the aesthetics of religious writings. In the passage which leads up to the chirograph-injuction section of his late sermon on Lamentations 3:1, Donne remarks that 'All the evills and mischiefes that light upon us in this world, come (for the most part) from this, *Quia fruimur utendis*, because we thinke to injoy those things which God hath given us to *use*.'⁵ The death of Christ, Donne continues, God proposed 'for our *use*, in this world, and we think to enjoy it' –

God would have us doe it over again, and we think it enough to know that Christ hath done it already; God would have us *write* it, and we doe onely *read* it; God would have us *practise* the death of Christ, and we do but *understand* it.

That Herbert chose not just to 'read it' but to 'write it' (as Donne would say) is clear enough: he practised the death of Christ in the chirograph of his poem. But the 'counter-statement' within the fact of the poem is that his art lures him into temptation, into enjoyment; and poetry should be *used* to find ultimate enjoyment. In his silence, as Herbert says in 'Frailtie,' he can 'surname' the '*honour, riches, or fair eyes*' of the materials of poetry but 'guilded clay.' But the 'Brave language' of his verse presents the love-song of the world, and 'That which was dust before, doth quickly rise, / And prick mine eyes': 'Affront those *joyes*,' he pleads, 'wherewith thou didst endow / And long since *wed* / My poore soul, ev'n *sick of love*.' Augustine himself had complained in his *Confessions* of the precarious balance of use and abuse in art: 'Thus vacillate I between dangerous pleasure and tried soundness ... Yet when it happens to me to be more moved by the singing than by what is sung, I confess myself to have sinned criminally, and then I would rather not have heard the singing.'⁶ *Use* means suspended enjoyment, and because of its tremendous capacity to be readily enjoyed rather than used, poetry remains for Herbert a dangerous tool. It damns him who 'loves amisse,' who loves the art for itself and 'This worlds delights before true Christian *joy*': 'The world an ancient murderer is; / Thousands of souls it hath and doth destroy / *With her enchanting voice*.'

'Suppose we were wanderers who could not live in blessedness except in home,' Augustine hypothesizes in *De Doctrina*, superimposing the figure of

Ulysses on the figure of the wayfarer-wanderer Christian pilgrim, 'miserable in our wandering and desiring to end it and to return to our native country'[7] –

We would need vehicles for land and sea which could be used to help us reach our homeland, which is to be enjoyed. But if the amenities of the journey and the motion of the vehicles itself delighted us, and we were led to enjoy those things which we should use, we should not wish to end our journey quickly, and, entangled in a perverse sweetness, we should be alienated from our country, whose sweetness would make us blessed. Thus in this mortal life, *wandering from God, if we wish to return to our native country where we can be blessed, we should use this world and not enjoy it.*

Poetry, quite simply, is the 'vehicle,' or 'vessel,' which Herbert employs as homesick wanderer *en route* to God ('while I *use* / I am with thee').[8] But its earthly beauty can shipwreck the traveller, entangling him in the false love, 'a sorrie wedding,' for that which is not worthy to be loved. We should 'use this world and not enjoy it,' Augustine explains, 'so that the "invisible things" of God "being understood by the things that are made" may be seen, that is, so that by means of corporal and temporal things we may comprehend the eternal and spiritual.' As the ear of the poet is prone to the temptations of the 'enchanting voice' of the world, so his eye is prey to seduction and diversion by 'the things that are made,' things which are abused only when they draw him away from rather than toward his home in 'the "invisible things" of God': 'That which was dust before, doth quickly rise, / *And prick mine eyes*,' Herbert confesses in 'Frailtie.' When the 'eye' commits itself to the corporal gold of earth, as in 'Self-condemnation,' it destroys its bearer-wanderer (the eye-I) on the rock of what is seen: 'Look back upon thine own estate, / Call *home* thine eye (that busie *wanderer*).'

Injunctions, emblem-tags, proverbs, and parables appear throughout *The Temple*, bearing a warning to the poet himself that as he is but a wanderer in this world travelling to God on a sea of words, so he must *use* those words: 'Call to minde thy dreame,' he concludes in 'The Size,' calling home his eye to a picture, 'An *earthly globe*, / On whose meridian was engraven, / *These seas are tears, and heav'n the haven.*' In its belittlement of earthly joy ('Modest and *moderate joyes* to those, that have / Title to more hereafter when they part'), 'The Size' is a very Augustinian poem: it echoes with the notion of proper and improper joy. 'Great joyes are all at once; / But little do reserve themselves for more,' 'Thy Saviour sentenc'd joy, / And in the flesh condemn'd it as unfit,' and 'we should count, / Since the last joy.' The lexical pattern is consistent with the journey image – 'Those are at home; these journey still, / And meet the rest on Sions hill.' But Herbert's own version of the Augustinian 'use and enjoyment' trope appropriates it to the nature of his poetry, accommodates it to the problem of transcendent art. Language itself is on the journey home; equivocal language does not rest here, in time, in single meaning – it finds no fixed harbour in single definition – for it only *uses* the oneness of earthly sound to convey the totality of God.

'I know the wayes of Learning,' Herbert begins in 'The Pearl,' the 'quick returns of courtesie and *wit*': 'When glorie swells the heart, and moldeth it / To all *expressions both of hand and eye*, / Which *on the world a true-love-knot may tie*.' The binding 'love-knot' which can chain the poet to the earthliness of his language (the 'sweet strains' – 'propositions of hot bloud and brains') is released in 'The Pearl' by transcendent love become flesh ('thy silk twist let down from heav'n to me') which transforms the poet's lexical preference for noun-things grounding him in earth ('The stock and surplus') into verb-motion which flies-aspires to heaven: 'Yet I love thee,' 'Yet I love thee,' 'Yet I love thee' – 'how by it / To climbe to thee.' The 'love-knot' on the world which pulls against the speaker's determination and destination ('Yet I love thee,' 'Yet I love thee,' 'Yet I love thee') is Augustinian 'cupidity' at war with its opposite, 'charity.' 'I call *charity*,' Augustine explains in a passage which explicates the journey of 'The Church' toward 'Love,' 'the motion of the soul toward the enjoyment of *God for his own sake*, and the enjoyment of one's self and one's neighbor *for the sake of God*; but "*cupidity*" is the motion of the soul toward the enjoyment of one's self, one's neighbor, or any corporal thing for the sake of something other than God.'[9] Understandably, '*for thy sake*' in 'The Elixir' is a 'tincture' which turns all to gold: 'Teach me, my God and King, / *In all things thee to see*,' Herbert begins in that poem. The 'charity' of the final 'Love' poem resolves the 'cupidity' of the first 'Love' poem. 'Our *eies* shall see thee, which before saw *dust*,' Herbert prophesies in 'Love (II)' of the ultimate goal of the soul in charity, released from its eyes for this world and its songs. 'Give up your *feet* and *running to mine eyes*,' Herbert urges his 'verses' in 'Grief': 'And keep your *measures* for some lovers lute.' Tears of repentance overcome the natural cupidity of song; they blind the eyes enamoured of the things that are visible and now, preparing them for their eschatological opening in God. And the flesh and dust of poetry – the stuff of suffering, of tormenting tension and distraction as in 'Frailtie' ('That which was *dust* before, doth quickly rise, / And prick mine *eyes*') – works finally to regain, through its tears, the vision of God: '*Summon all the dust to rise*, / Till it stirre, and *rubbe the eyes*' ('Doomsday').

Thinking in Renaissance England is, of course, a multilingual proposition; this is something which has been absorbed and used by Milton criticism more than it has been by the criticism of the lyric poetry of the time. Augustine's Latin for 'enjoy,' '*frui*,' extends itself etymologically through Herbert's imagery (and the thought behind it) of 'leaves,' 'buds,' and '*fruition*.' 'Sunday' is univocally 'the *fruit* of this, the next worlds *bud*': it is the type of fruition-enjoyment in the world to come. 'There is no *fruitfull* yeare,' Herbert claims unambiguously in his poem (on his way) 'Home': 'but that which brings / The *last and lov'd*, though dreadful day.' The clarity and simplicity of the '*frui*' of the end in 'Home' ('*no* fruitfull yeare *but*'), prefigured by the obscure univocacy (two words, one meaning) of the '*fruit*'-'*bud*' of 'Sunday,' contrasts itself sharply with the equivocacy (one word, two meanings) of the '*frui*' of 'worky-daie' time. A 'sonne' is both '*light and fruit*': ' a *fruitfull* flame / Chasing the fathers dimnesse.' The 'sun,' then, of earthly sound and sight, the *homonym* of the world's enchanting voice and carnal joy, is converted to *use*: it is *used* to light the way to 'fruit' (fruition-enjoyment in the Father). The homonymous-equivocal word is the 'vessel' which carries the earthly wanderer home to final meaning in God. Thus, equivocacy is the mode and idiom of 'The Church' in time, at once on earth and in heaven, *two in one*; equivocal language is *used*, as the word 'sonne,' and as the Son making known the Father, in order to be *enjoyed* in its 'fruit' above. 'Yet *one*, if good, may *title to a number*,' Herbert reasons in 'An Offering': '*single* things grow *fruitfull* by deserts.' The 'use and enjoyment' dynamics of equivocal language in 'The Church' present themselves as an offering, and single words aspire to fruition. 'Each thing that is, although in *use* and *name* / It go for one,' we hear similarly in 'Providence,' 'hath many wayes in store / To honour thee.'

In the final view of 'The Church,'[10] language is not rejected for its carnal-audible-sensual-visible-*usable* part, but the 'enchanting voice' of its formal and temporal expression must be monitored and remembered for what it is: now-use and later-joy *at once*. '*Lovely* enchanting language,' Herbert resolves of the *charitable* function of the enchantment of human voice and the lure of its song in 'The Forerunners.'[11] As the 'fruitfull *flame*' of the sun-Son, the earthly beauty of 'sweet phrases' works to draw men towards the second element of their equivocacy (the 'Beautie' in 'beauteous words'): 'True beautie dwells on high: *ours is a flame* / But borrow'd thence *to light us thither*.' The beauty of poetry which is 'use' is accusative in structure, for such beauty comes equivocally *into* the sound of the voice, '*lovely* metaphors,' in order to bring man as subject back *into* the object of his action and restless wandering – into the *loveliness* of God. Equivocacy is the idiom of eternity-come-*into*-time, of the Incarnation and the eternal mystery of two-become-one. Whereas univocacy, 'fruit'-'bud,' is the journey *up* the ladder *Immanuel* to pure meaning outside sound and time, equivocacy is the second motion of the angels down that ladder into the enacted meaning and enduring tension of the 'measures' of verse. Equivocacy offers a recapitulation of the paradigm rendered by the Incarnation: man and God *in one.*

II *INVENIRE*: BEAUTY IN DISCOVERY

It is too bad, from one point of view, that twentieth-century criticism of seventeenth-century poetry has stressed the influence of an Augustine adapted to the ideas of the Reformation. For the Augustine who is encountered without the Reformation filter is an Augustine who preached above all else the meaning of the Incarnation and its continued meaning as spirit takes *form.* The 'body' and the 'Body,' the lexical signatures of St Augustine, are the evidence of his own hard-come-by case against Platonism. While we are in time, abstract nouns should not remove themselves from their particular forms, grace should not forget the graceful, vehicle remains in time the embodiment of tenor, and, in Herbert's words, 'Beautie and beauteous words should go together.'

Concerned with time, concerned with the *measure* of time which is to become Herbert's '*In you* Redemption measures all my time,' St Augustine comes across as a theologian concerned above all else with the *descent* of the Creator into the flesh of his creation and its history. *Two become one, two into one,* or *two in one* is a trope central to the writing of St Augustine. And it is a figure of thought most congenial to the equivocacy of the poetic language of George Herbert: two meanings in one. The work of St Augustine cries out with the suffering incumbent on the necessity of God becoming one with man (as does the poetry of Herbert). But nowhere are the optative expressions of desire for release from that tortured condition ('Oh loose this frame, knot of man untie! / That my free soul may use her wing') counted as anything but declamation against what is and must be.

'Lord, in thee,' Herbert concludes in the second of the sonnets to his mother, 'The *beauty* lies in the *discovery.*' If we trace back the origin of the word 'discovery' ('*inventio*'), Augustine remarks, 'what else does it mean, than that to discover is to *come into that which is sought*?'[12] For Herbert and for Augustine, a right understanding of *invention* is offered by its root, *invenire,* a 'coming into' and '*discovery*'; and what is sought (and discovered) is not the surface of the art itself but God. *Poor invention,* Herbert's sonnet complains, is that which 'doth not upward go / To praise': it is a fire which '*burns in their low mind.*' That which reduces itself to form alone *abuses* the schemes and tropes of the commonplace book of God's creation:

Each cloud distills thy praise and doth forbid
Poets to turn it to another *use*:
Roses and *Lillies* speak thee; and to make
A pair of Cheeks of them, is thy *abuse*.

God's places should not be 'pulled from' but they should come into their own
in art. Beauty, for Herbert, is God's meeting with the *topoi*, the efficient
causes of art; beauty is the 'discovery' of God himself within the storehouses
of schemes and tropes. Quaint words themselves are not 'sought out' with
'trim invention' ('Jordan II'), but God himself is found there in all the dust-
wit and lusty flesh of poetry.

Language, as life, has 'a *double* motion,' an equivocal destiny ('My *words*
& thoughts do both express this notion'): '*One* life is *In* flesh, and tends to
earth: / *The other* winds towards *Him*, whose happie birth / Taught me to live
here so, *That* still one eye / Should aim and shoot at that which *Is* on high.' To
suggest that the '*Is*' of Being completely discards the '*In*' of flesh is to misread
Herbert's poetry and to deny his poetic celebration of the continuing mystery
of the Incarnation. 'The Church' is *about* the presence of God *in his Body*: it
is a re-presentation of 'Sublime *Wisedome*, and humble *Flesh*, made one
Person,' as one Augustinian-minded thinker, William Austin, puts it in 1621.
'*Ut, ubi Humilitas, ibi & Sapientia*.'[13]

Beauty is found, according to Augustine, in the 'fitness,' 'likeness,' and
'equality' of God and His Image, in neither the one nor the other alone (if
either could be found 'alone' – 'So both each are each, and all in each, and each
in all, and all in all, and all are one');[14] beauty is in the *relation* of the earthly
and the heavenly parts, and the relatedness itself is the aesthetic of 'discovery.'
'Therefore that unspeakable *conjunction* of the Father and His image is not
without *fruition*, without *love*, without *joy*,' Augustine writes,

Therefore that love, delight, felicity, or blessedness, if indeed it can be worthily expressed by any human word, is called by him, in short, *Use*; and is the Holy Spirit in
the Trinity, not begotten, but the *sweetness of the begetter and of the begotten*, filling
all creatures.[15]

Beauty is found at the meeting point of God and 'the good fellowship of
dust' ('Church-monuments'). And the earth-dust-ground of the humility
('*humus*'-'earth') of flesh is the '*heavenly Ladder*, by which our God *de-
scended* to Earth.'[16] The 'hallow'd fire' of Herbert's invention indeed meets
with the 'lowly matter' of earth and clay ('The Priesthood'), but it makes
'curious things' of 'wretched earth' and rises upward, 'since God doth vessels

often make / Of lowly matter *for high uses meet.*' Earth is not separate from but made one with truth in the mystery of the equivocal relatedness of 'The Sonne': 'So in *one word* our Lords *humilitie* / We turn upon him in a sense most true.' As beauty is a 'coming into' of earth-heaven, man-God, humility-wisdom ('the sweetness of the begetter and of the begotten'), the 'beauteous words' of 'The Church' achieve '*a sweet content*'; language is '*A speaking sweet,*' and the 'call' is but a *usefull* 'breathing of the sweet.'

As Herbert's adaptation of Augustine's 'use and enjoyment' theory expresses itself in *fruition* imagery, so his belief in *beauty as discovery* grounds itself in the topic of *what can be made of earth* and the collocated craftsmanship and husbandry imagery. Earth-ground-dust and 'our Lords humility' are the places of Herbert's invention and the *topoi* which beauty *comes into*: earth is 'fitted by the fire and trade / Of skilfull artists.' Although Herbert begins in doubt at the prospect of the meanness of his *topoi* of rhetorical amplification, of 'Comparing dust with dust, and earth with earth' ('Church Monuments'), he ends by 'discovery' in 'The Priesthood' that the earth-clay of the 'meane stuffe' is God's 'vessel'; that beauty is 'found out' of earth, 'So that at once both feeder, dish, and meat / Have *one beginning and one finall summe.*' Earth is the *place* where the begetter is discovered in the begotten, and so, 'I do not greatly wonder at the sight, / If *earth in earth delight.*' Here natural cupidity is transformed into charity by poetry, for from the ground of humility and the water of sorrow grows the flower, *Nazareth*, which is art. God '*found me on the ground,*' Herbert recalls in 'The Banquet.' The *feast* of God *in man* and the 'sweetnesse' of the *conjunction* of God and man *in one another*, equivocally as the other, is the 'beauty' which is 'discovered' in Herbert's poetry: 'Onely God, who gives perfumes, / *Flesh assumes,* / And with it perfumes my heart.' As Herbert's aesthetic rests satisfied with earth-flesh as one aspect of its equivocal (one-both) nature, as it accepts its carnality not for 'enjoyment' but for 'use,' it turns to the action of the body, the gesture of the flesh, as the initiator and sustainer of the dynamics of worship: '*I throw me at his feet*' ('The Priesthood').

III   ON EARTH AS IT IS IN HEAVEN

Six years after the death of George Herbert, William Laud in a 'Conference' with Mr Fisher explained that 'the *Inward Worship* of the Heart, is the *Great Service of God*' but that 'the *Externall worship* of God in his Church is the *Great Witnesse* to the World, that Our heart stands right in that *Service of God*' –

For of that which is *Inward* there can be no *Witnesse* among men, nor no *Example* for men. Now no Externall Action in the world can be *Uniforme* without some *Ceremonies* ... And scarce any Thing hath hurt *Religion* more in these broken Times, then an Opinion in too many men, That because *Rome* had thrust some Unnecessary, and many Superstitious Ceremonies upon the Church, therefore the *Reformation* must have none at all; Not considering therewhile, That *Ceremonies* are the *Hedge* that fence the *Substance of Religion* from all the Indignities, which *Prophanenesse* and *Sacriledge* too Commonly put upon it. [17]

Laud's impassioned apology for the necessity of the use of the body and external ceremony does not stand alone in the Anglican theology of the seventeenth century. In his *Notes on the Book of Common Prayer*, John Cosin defends ceremony on the basis of its function as Example – 'The end which is aimed at in setting down the outward form of all religious actions, is the edification of the Church'[18] – and he addresses the contentious issue of the Prayer-Book's 'kneeling' rubric, after the consecration of the Sacrament, at some length. Since, he argues, 'the Body and blood of Christ are sacramentally and really (not feignedly) present, when the blessed Bread and Wine are taken by the faithful communicants,'

the adoration is then and there given to Christ Himself, neither is nor ought to be directed to any sensible object, such as are the blessed elements. But our kneeling, and the outward gesture of humility and reverence in our bodies, is ordained only to testify and express the inward reverence and devotion of our souls towards our blessed Saviour, who vouchsafed to sacrifice Himself for us upon the Cross, and now presenteth Himself to be united sacramentally to us. [19]

Laud's 1637 Star Chamber message distinguishes the nature of proper bodily adoration this way: 'I say, *adoring at* the *Sacrament*, not *adoring* the *Sacrament*.'[20] And that brief comment in 1637 is but a condensation of a more elaborate argument voiced by Thomas Cestren as early as 1618: in the opinion of some, 'the Papists *adore*,' he explains, 'the Element of *bread*, as the very person of the Son of God.' But such is not the position of the English Church:

Here you have a gesture of *Adoration*, I say not to the *Cup*; but, at the receiving of the *Cup*, unto *Christ*, by relation of a *gift*, from a *Giver*: I say againe unto *Christ*; for that *Adoration* was directed unto him, unto whom the oration and prayer was due, in saying, *Amen*.[21]

Puritan railing against the evils of external ceremony in worship can be both vituperative and humorously irrational. Thus, Peter Smart, for instance, writes from Edinburgh in 1628 of John Cosin's 'speculative and theoretical Popery.' Claiming that Cosin has set up Angels 'round the quire of Durham Church,' Smart labels all ceremonies 'vanities' – '*Those vanities*, saith a learned interpreter, are *humane traditions, superstitious Ceremonies, which undermine and overthrow both the Law and the Gospell.*'[22] The Nonconformists had their 'reasons,' recognizably consistent 'Opinions' which were, as the Anglicans understood them to be: that there should be no ceremony without the warrant of Christ, that no human ceremony should be appropriated to God's worship, that there should be no mystical significance in any thing, that no ceremony should be used which had once been 'superstitiously abused,' and that no bodily gesture at the Lord's Supper is lawful.[23] But the entire mode of the conservative Anglicans is rational; weighing everything in their characteristic idiom, 'on the one hand, on the other,' the vast majority wrote as did John Gauden in the 1660s that 'nothing of the *Romish corruption* in *Doctrine*, or *Superstition* in Devotion, was reteined in our *English Liturgy*, which took nothing either of *Doctrine* out of it but what was first in the *Scriptures*' –

nor did the Church of *England* retain any *ceremonies*, as the *Crosse, Surplice, Standing up at the Creed*, or *Kneeling at the Lords Supper*, but what were above a *thousand* years old ... evident in the *Histories, Councils* and *Fathers* of the first 600. years.[24]

Without ceremonies, Gauden argues, 'the most *sacred* and *venerable mysteries* must be exposed to that *rudenesse* and *unpreparednesse*, that *barrennesse* and *superficialnesse*, that *defect* and *deformity*, both for matter and manner, judgment and expression'; ceremonies 'preserve the truth of Christian and Reformed *Doctrine*,' a liturgy 'is necessary for the *harmony* and sweet communion of all Christians, in *National* as well as *Parochial Churches*,' it provides 'benefit and comfort,' and it 'conduceth to the *edification* and *salvation* as well as unanimity and peace in the *meaner sort of people*; to whom daily *variety of expressions* in *prayer*, or *Sacraments*, is much at one with *Latin Service*; little understood, and lesse remembered by them.'[25]

The judiciousness of the Anglican attitude toward ceremony, of course, begins with the 1549 'Of Ceremonies' included in the 1549 Prayer-Book, a piece of literature in which St Augustine and his language of 'use and abuse' figure prominently. Explaining 'why some of the accustomed Ceremonies be put away, and some retained and kept still,' the document conjectures and muses, 'But what would Saint Augustine have said, if he had seen the Ceremonies of late days used among us?' Those ceremonies must 'be taken away which were most *abused*,' the document maintains, although 'without some Ceremonies it is not possible to keep any Order, or quite Discipline in the Church.' From that 'on the one hand, on the other' position grew both extremes of seventeenth-century England. In his *Notes on the Book of Common Prayer*, Lancelot Andrewes wrote beside that 'Of Ceremonies,' '*Ceremonias definiunt* 1. *Decorum* 2. *Disciplina* 3. *Significatio.*'[26] And his own annotation on its complaint, 'That they would innovate all things,' reacts conservatively, capturing well the point of view which will be expressed by the poetry of George Herbert: '*Non est innovatio dicenda, si quid in melius simpliciter, seu alteratione, seu adjectione fiat.*'[27] Although they are but brief notes, the comments which Andrewes makes about the official line of the Church in 1549 provide an interesting transition into his prescriptions in *A Preparation to Prayer*. Referring all to Scripture itself, Andrewes insists, '*We must* at the time of prayer bow down our knees, as our Saviour Christ did [Luke 22:41] –

We must 'lift up our hearts with our hands' [Lamentations 3:41]. Our eyes must be lifted up to God 'That dwelleth in the heaven' [Psalm 123:1]. And, as David says, all our 'bones' must be exercised in prayer.[28]

There is no ambiguity here. Neither is there any ambiguity in the total corpus of the poetry of George Herbert. 'The Method' begins in bodily gesture: 'Then once more pray: / *Down with thy knees, up with thy voice.*'

Before looking at the evidence we have of what must have been Herbert's own attitude toward the proper use of the gestures of the body and their meaning in *The Temple*, we do well, given our context, to keep in mind the elaborately *logical* comments Andrewes makes on the Lord's Prayer (Luke 11:1) and, particularly, on what Andrewes considers to be its central phrase, '*On Earth as it is in Heaven.*' For in the concept, *on earth as in heaven*, rests the sacramentality of Herbert's poetry and the basis of the authority for bodily gesture. Christ himself, Andrewes explains, 'is both in heaven and earth' –

for as He is called 'the Head of His Church' [Ephesians 1:22] He is in heaven, but in respect of His body Which is called Christ [Corinthians 12:27] He is on earth, that is, the Church, may do God's will, even as Christ the Head Who is in heaven hath done it.[29]

That we may be 'heavens living on earth' (Romans 10:18), Andrewes continues, we must seek to bring the *flesh into subjection*, 'that our old man and outward man may conform himself to the inward and new man.' As it bows and buckles itself to the ground-earth appropriate to the 'terrene part,' then, the body is subjected to the rule of the soul, 'celestial part.' And, hence, there is an unassailable logic to 'The Method': when he goes *down on his knees* and up with his voice, the poet will bring *heaven to earth*, and, thus, '*God* will say, / *Glad heart rejoyce.*'

'The Countrey Parson,' Herbert begins in 'The Parson praying,' '*composeth himselfe to all possible reverence*': 'lifting up his heart and hands, and eyes, and *using all other gestures* which may expresse a hearty, and unfeyned devotion.' It should be clear that by the time he wrote *The Country Parson* Herbert had adopted, perhaps gone back to, the attitude toward ceremony set forth by his old teacher, Lancelot Andrewes. Convincing because of its beauty bearing the mark of the man, there is also the story told by Walton of Herbert's Induction, which suggests something of the depth of Herbert's belief in the significance of physical gesture: 'he was shut into *Bemerton* Church, being left there alone to Toll the Bell, (as the Law requires him:)' –

he staid so much longer than an ordinary time, before he return'd to those Friends that staid expecting him at the Church-door, that his friend, Mr. *Woodnot*, look'd in at the Church-window, and *saw him lie prostrate on the ground before the Altar:* at which time and place (as he after told Mr. *Woodnot*) he set some Rules to himself, for the future manage of his life.[30]

But there is also considerable reference to gesture in *The Temple* itself, and it is there that our otherwise simply academic interest in the degree to which Herbert believed in the effectuality of the use of the body in the worship of God becomes of crucial interpretive importance. Many of the poems not in the Williams MS present the *picture* of the poet praying as an integral part of the prayer. '*With doubling knees* and weary bones, / ... To thee my sighs, my tears ascend,' Herbert complains in 'Longing.' And '*My knees pierce th'earth*, mine eies the skie,' he reports of his actions in 'The Search.' The narratives of both poems, which begin with the subjection of the flesh, bring Herbert, in each case, to some re-cognition of *heaven on earth*. 'Lord Jesu, thou didst bow / Thy dying head upon the tree: / Be not now / More dead to me,' Herbert resolves in 'Longing,' identifying himself iconographically with *Immanuel*. 'So doth thy nearnesse bear the bell, / *Making two one*,' Herbert concludes of the ultimate equivocacy of Head and Body, heaven and earth, in 'The Search.'

Man's nature resembles the two-and-one character of equivocacy; and therefore, Andrewes reasons, 'man (being a creature consisting of *body* and *soule*) should serve his Creator with both.'[31] Man 'is compounded of soul and body: and the worship of God, and prayer to God, is an act of the soul; which the body by the senses thereof may divert the mind from, but cannot help it forwards, *till by the motion and gesture of the body the soul be engaged to attend on that which the mind proposeth,*' Herbert Thorndike argues in 1659 of the psychology of gesture in prayer.[32] In order to be 'as one' in the oneness of God, in order to discover the atonement of man and God, heaven and earth, in Christ and as Christ ('Making two one'), the poet-priest of *The Temple* acknowledges ceremony as 'not onely innocent, but reverend.' Gesture brings Herbert into communion with the Body of Christ as the action of the body is presented in imitation of Christ: 'our *Saviour Christ,*' Andrewes instructs in his *Institutiones Piae*, '(every one of whose *actions* ought to be a *rule* to us) sometimes *fell on his face*, sometimes *kneeled*, and sometimes *lifted up his eyes* when he prayed.'[33] When 'I find my Saviour *falling* on his *face* [Matthew 26:39],' John Prideaux reasons considerably later (1655), 'I should hold him far from superstition, that in *time* and *place*, and where it may be fitly performed, shall prostrate his whole *body* ... in adoring *him in whose book are all our members written.*'[34]

Herbert's Augustinianism does not reject the carnal man and the carnality of poetry but *uses* it to find the spiritual man, that One Man whose identity is to be recognized by His Body.[35] Outward voice (and the carnality of poetry), similarly, is the place where Beauty resides: 'The very *dust*, where thou dost tread and go, / Makes beauties here' ('Dulnesse'). Augustine's *verbum vocis* is 'come into,' 'discovered,' by *verbum cordis*.[36] And it is thus that things are done *on earth as they are in heaven:* the outward and the inward expressions of man are joined equivocally *as one* in the mystery of *our old man, nailed to the Cross*. It is the subjection of the body and its voice (its 'throwing under' – on the ground) as crucified flesh, in 'Thy bloudy death,' which makes for 'Pure red and white.' He that undervalues '*outward things*, in the religious service of God,' John Donne confesses in one of his less anti-Roman moments, 'though he begin at *ceremoniall* and *rituall* things, will come quickly to call *Sacraments* but outward things, and *Sermons*, and *publique prayers*, but outward things, in contempt.'[37] Praise, for Herbert at the end of the spiritual journey in 'The Church,' is both to '*mean and speak*': 'when I did *call*, / Thou heardst my call, *and more*.' Predicating itself by its limit and the category of 'quantity,' *verbum vocis* in Herbert's final 'Praise' poem defines, *by its very limitations*, what is '*more*' in the *verbum cordis* of the One new man: 'yet of a size / That would *contain much more*,' 'The glasse was *full and more*,' 'Both all my praise, *and more*.'

Sacramental when they are not enjoyed but *used*,[38] then, both the gestures of the body and the outward expression of the body's voice in verse are for Herbert the *topoi* of man's 'discovery' as/in God. Herbert's 'A true Hymne' has frequently annotated the arguments of those who stress Herbert's Protestantism, associated, as it is, with the Augustinianism of the Reformation. As I read it, the lexical emphasis on the word 'heart' is beyond doubt ('My heart was meaning all the day,' and 'Whereas if th'heart be moved'), but there is another side to the coin which is, simply, that 'A true Hymne' is liturgical; it is a *set prayer: 'My joy, my life, my crown!'* Herbert frequently turns to liturgical *set form*, held by the 'Puritans' to be in opposition to expressions from the heart, as the *locus* of his own poetic. Thus, in 'Jordan (1),' his poetry contents itself with the '*My God, My King*' of the liturgically appropriated Psalms; and structure in 'The Forerunners' turns on the set form of a liturgical refrain, '*Thou art still my God.*' Herbert's demonstrable belief in the validity of set form as expression not of individual but of *whole self in Church* aligns him, once again, with Lancelot Andrewes and those later who were to uphold the need for 'set forms of Liturgy' and outward expression in the 1660s. Calling the carnality of the forms and bodily worship in liturgy a 'necessary hedge' (as had Andrewes before him), Henry Hammond broods over 'the no-form being as fitly accommodated to the no-Church, as the no-hedge, no-wall to the Common, or desert, the no-inclosure to the no-plantation.'[39] Similarly, referring to 'Prayers, Praises, and *Sacramental* celebrations' as 'the great *characters* and confirmation of true Christians communion with God, with their Saviour, and the blessed Spirit,' John Gauden deplores the 'strange and unheard *Ostracisme* in many Congregations of England' imposed on the set form of prayer commended to us by Christ himself: such negligence makes way for 'the *contagion* and *deformity* of private Ministers frequent infirmities, either in their *invention, judgment, memory or utterance.*'[40]

Contrary to the prevailing opinion now, both 'plainness' and 'truth' could be found in the vocal expression of the carnal man in set form, according to Anglican theory of the time. Without a *form* for expression the heart only *tries* ('means') to say ('Somewhat it *fain would say*: / And still it runneth *mutt'ring* up and down'). Outward form provides a meeting place for subject and object ('*I love*' – '*Loved*'); there heaven is brought to earth, *equivocated as earth*, confining itself to limit but arguing, thereby, '*and more.*' 'Whatsoever prayers we make ourselves they have some earth,' Andrewes argues in preparation for a statement about the uniqueness of the Lord's Prayer, 'because we ourselves are of the earth, but the prayer instituted by Christ is free from all imperfection, because *it was penned from Him That was "from above"* [John 3:31].'[41] The Lord's Prayer, according to Andrewes, is the *topos* which equivocates the 'mean' and the 'say,' the 'sign,' and the 'speak,' the '*cogitate*' and the '*dicite*' of praise. As such, it is the type of Herbert's poetry; it is the '*love*' condescending to flesh and form, a love which must be '*copied*' as the '*sweetnesse*' has been '*readie penn'd*.' It is not enough, Andrewes insists, 'to thinke in our minds this prayer, but our prayers must be vocal … as we ourselves have not only a soul but a body also, *so our prayer must have a body;* our "tongue must be the pen of a ready writer" [Psalm 45:1].' Outward form, like language of Herbert, is 'neat' ('How *neatly* do we give *one only name* / To parents issue and the sunnes bright starre!'): the form-flesh of 'parents issue' (both *body* and *Fall*) is reconciled to and in the 'starre' of heaven by redemptive equivocacy where *one* contains and entertains *more*.

'My *flesh* and *bones* and *joynts* do pray: / And ev'n my *verse*,' Herbert sorrows in 'Home': verse itself is a gesture of the body and it submits itself to rule, *copying* heaven onto earth. Homonym honours the outward word, the sound of the word, as the domicile of meaning. As equivocacy predicates without an equative verb (such as 'is' or 'becomes'), it 'sayes' much more than the structure of its prose indicates. The word, '*Stay*, sayes ever, *Come*,' only by virtue of the fact that the system of Herbert's poetic language in *The Temple* need not always render the transforming copula ('Stay *is* Come' or 'Stay *equals* Come'): the predicate is embodied in the subject; it is included in the outward form of one word which is the subject of an unspoken proposition. So bodily gesture, 'Down with thy knees,' is an unspoken predication of not just what 'is' but Being which is above the constrictions of proposition.

At the risk of stressing the part of form and flesh in Herbert's poetry too much over the part of the spirit and the silence of the heart, I have tried here to restore one element of its basic equivocacy (one = two) which has, in the final balance of things, been too long forgotten by Herbert criticism.[42] The point is that his poetry is neither one thing nor the other alone; it is about the reconciliation of spirit and flesh as healed and *whole*, and it praises the God who made of *two folds one*. On the external, the formal, the liturgical, a man 'may stay his eye,' or 'if he pleaseth, through it passe, / And then the heav'n espie.' Heaven is found *in* the glass through which we now see darkly, and it is the 'sweet content' of (*in*) the crucified body of form which comprises the accusative equivocacy found in 'The Church.' What is more (and this, again, is the *balance* of equivocacy's predication), it is not just that the spirit is within the form but that the form is within the spirit, that there is *in love* a *sweetness ready penned*. Time and eternity meet there, and there the 'time to come is gone': 'He is thy night at noon: he is at night / Thy noon alone.' In writing, Augustine observes in his commentary on Psalm 45:1 ('*My tongue is the pen of a writer writing rapidly'*),[43] 'letter is written after letter; syllable after syllable; word after word' –

But there is nothing can exceed the swiftness, where there are not several words; and yet there is not any thing omitted; *since in the One are contained all things.*

Among the precepts of 'The Church-porch' we hear, 'If studious, *copie fair, what time hath blurr'd*; / *Redeem truth* from his jaws.' The chirograph of George Herbert enables the One to meet with all in Christ's fair copy on earth, and that fair copy is, on the one hand, but the dust-earth which 'measures' time yet, on the other, '*the six-daies world transposing in an houre.*'

IV SYNECDOCHE: THE PART AND THE WHOLE

Ellipsis is without doubt one of the most marked stylistic characteristics of Herbert's poetry. It is especially evident in the early poems of 'The Church' where the apparent disjunctions in thought affect the rhythm of the verse with repeated caesura: 'I go to Church; help me to wings, I / Will thither flie' –

> Man is all weaknesse; there is no such thing
> > As Prince or King:
> His arm is short; yet with a sling
> > He may do more. ('Praise i')

Dismemberment and discontinuity can be *seen* in the fissures in the hiero-glyph of the verse as well. And in 'Praise (ii)' we move into still another kind of disconnection, not so immediately apparent, as we jump in tense structure from future to past to future to past ('I will love thee' – 'Thou hast heard me' – 'I will sing thee' – 'Thou didst cleare me') in each stanza, experiencing at the same time alternating shifts in grammatical subject from first to second to first person ('I' – 'Thou' – 'I' – 'Thou'). The poem resolves itself in the tenseless infinitive which does not take a subject ('Small it is, in this poore sort / To enroll thee: / Ev'n eternitie is too short / To extoll thee'), and it prepares the way for the preponderance of 'when' clauses which create the concatenation of 'Praise (ii)' and which end ellipsis: 'But *when* mine eyes / Did weep to heav'n, they found a bottle there / ... Readie to take them in.'

What I suggest is that one of the maturing processes that *The Temple* records is the persona's growth into philosophical-theological understanding of the validity of synecdoche, of the part standing for the whole. Units of thought which remain a-part and dis-integrated in the first poems of 'The Church' conflate and translate into one another as the persona advances toward his own *wholeness* in and as 'The Church,' a member for the whole. 'O that I might some other hearts convert,' Herbert exclaims optatively at the end of his third 'Praise' poem, *'And so take up at use good store.'* The desire to convert others is no extraneous wish in Herbert's poetry self-indulgently tacked on to the poem: it is a part of the logic of 'The Church' and the dynamic relationship that obtains therein between any part and the whole; invention rests ('take up at use good store') in the discovery by the part of the whole.

The coat on which the lots were cast, Augustine comments in his *On the Gospel of John*, 'signifies *the unity of all the parts*, which is contained in the *bond of charity*': 'no one is excluded from a share thereof, who is discovered to belong to the whole.'[44] Theory of the relationship between the part and the whole became crucial in Reformation England when it became of utmost importance to the political theory of the Church in the time of its extreme troubles between 1640 and 1660. But even as early as 1628 William Laud preached a sermon at the opening of Parliament on March 17 maintaining that 'the ready way to out *Religion*, is to breake the *Unitie* of it' – 'And the Church and Commonwealth, take them severally, or together, they are, they can be no otherwise *One* then *Unione multorum*, by the uniting and agreeing of many in one.'[45] The Church, like the Commonwealth, Laud contends in that sermon, is 'as one Cittie, yet such a one (saith *Saint Augustine*) *cui est periculosa dissentio*, as to whom all breach of Unity is full of danger.' Arguing the case for the ecclesiastical non-conformers in 1684, Richard Baxter employs logic to answer the charge that they were separate and apart from the whole. 'We say, that the word "Church" used for the "Universal" and the "Particular," ' he testifies, 'is not *univocally* used, but *analogically, expenuria nominum*. As oft the *whole* and the *part* have one Name.'[46] A 'particular' church and the 'universal' church are *one* analogically and equivocally, Baxter concludes; and synecdoche is a form of equivocacy,[47] predicating the whole by the part (two in one).

'Sanguine, dicere asserit *Augustinus* ad Orosium, Quaest. 49. Quare duo hic egregia habemus. 1. *Universam Ecclesiam participem esse Calicis*. 2. Cum accipint dicere, Amen': so read the notes of Lancelot Andrewes on the 'Prayer of Consecration.'[48] The Universal Church is a partaking of the Cup. The philosophical theory of the function of synecdoche, of the equivocal predication of the Universal Church and the One Man as the whole by a part, affects Herbert's political relationship with his reader (requiring him to *convert* the reader into the whole). But synecdoche is also a constituent in the sacramentality of Herbert's language itself: the Head is one with the Body, 'The

Church,' as the part is with another part of the whole. Although he begins a-part from the whole, where he can effect nothing ('To write a verse or two is all the praise, / That I can raise: / ... *help me to wings*'), the speaker blossoms into an understanding of himself as that whole, 'essentiated' (to use a term from Baxter) as the Church: 'Having raised me to look up, / *In a cup*' –

> Sweetly he doth *meet my taste.*
> But I still being low and short,
>   Farre from court
> *Wine becomes a wing* at last.

Part and whole meet in the Cup of which a par-taking is the Church, and the speaker is freed to *enjoy* the wholeness which expresses itself as action ('he doth meet'), sense ('my taste'), and distance ('raised me'), and as transcendent predication: 'Wine *becomes* a wing at last.'

As he learns the effectuality of synecdoche ('*impart* the matter *wholly*') and the logic by which the highly equivocal 'part' ('So many joyes I writ down for my part') actuates and is actuated in the whole ('since all musick is but three parts vied / And multiplied'), the speaker predicates the syncretism of body and soul, gesture and heart, in synergetic language which lends a body to the soul. 'O that thou shouldst give dust a tongue / To crie to thee,' Herbert exclaims in 'Deniall': 'all day long *my heart was in my knee.*' The 'heart' endowed with the 'knee' of ceremonious gesture appears again proverbially in 'Businesse': 'Who in heart not ever kneels, / Neither sinne nor Saviour feels.' Most interesting of all, perhaps, is the heart-body syncretism of 'The Size,' where the speaker's instructions to the heart give it another body prosopopoeically ('Wherefore *sit down, good heart*, / Grasp not at much') and in that newly actuated body meet both eternity and time, joy and use: 'For we should count, *Since the last joy.*' As the poet's failure to recognize the implications of the validity of philosophical synecdoche prevents him from relating part to part in 'Praise (II)' ('In my heart, though not in heaven, / I can raise thee'), so his understanding of that lesson in philosophical grammar releases him into whole man, whole time, whole Church (where he flies): 'Here is a *joy* that drowneth quite / Your delight, / *As a floud the lower grounds.*'

Although the hermeneutic difficulties in assessing the exact nature of Herbert's Augustinianism are extensive indeed, I think the point is worth making that the possibilities are not limited to the Augustine who had read St Paul. The 'Of Ceremonies' of the English Church and the Sacramental articles of that Church's faith are saturated with the influence of an Augustine who had thought judiciously about the real and phenomenological relation between the inner man and his outer world. Both 'inner' and 'outer' are but parts of the whole as are, for that matter, enjoyment and use. Joy, which is of the Trinity alone, *comes into* use, participating and partaking as Trinitarian activity in the world of time: 'I felt a sugred strange delight, / Passing all cordials made by any art, / *Bedew, embalme, and overrunne* my heart, / And take *it in.*' If there was ever a problem which haunted St Augustine, it was the problem of time-eternity and its relation to human speech. The last chapters of Book Eleven of the *Confessions*[49] ('We seem by the space of a short syllable to measure the space of a long syllable' – 'I measure not the future, for it is not yet; nor do I measure the past, because it no longer is,' etc.) may very well be the source of Herbert's equivocal 'measure' concept of his poetry. And if this is so, philosophical synecdoche may be the single most important aspect of the thought of St Augustine to have shown its distinctive influence on Herbert's poetry. Augustine's heavy reliance on memory in his resolution of the problem of the time-measures of speech is probably an historical explanation, too, of what has recently been noticed to be the 'redoubling' phenomenon in his poetry:[50] 'I am about to repeat a psalm I know,' Augustine posits in conclusion,

Before I begin, my attention is extended to the whole; but when I have begun, as much of it as becomes past by my saying it is extended to my memory ... the memory is enlarged, until the whole expectation be exhausted, when that whole action being ended shall have passed into memory. And what takes place in the entire psalm, takes place also in each individual part of it, and in each individual syllable; this holds in the longer action, of which the psalm is perhaps a portion; the same holds in the *whole life of man, of which all the actions of men are parts.*[51]

Logically, synecdoche (whether grammatical, temporal, ecclesiastical, and/or sacramental) is a form of *relation* which draws together, into one another and as the other, the part and the whole. As Herbert uses it, synecdoche is sacramental, for it obtains not only a 'significant' but an 'obsignant' relation between the part and the whole, 'sealing and exhibiting unto us the Truth of Gods promise' in that whole.[52] The 'sugred strange delight' both comes into and takes into; and man's 'partial' speech is made, thereby, the sacred 'traffick' and 'commerce' of 'The Odour.' The words '*My Master*' bear the 'sweet content' of the whole of which the words '*My servant*' are a part (by way of *relation*, as 'father' and 'son'): 'For when *My Master*, which alone is sweet, / And ev'n in my unworthinesse pleasing, / *Shall call and meet*, / *My servant* ... / That call is but the breathing of the sweet.' Synecdoche progresses into the totality of synaesthetic experience ('This broth of smells') when it is understood as a relation, '*not changed in substance, but in use*; as it is in other *Relations*': 'What cordials make this curious broth.'

4

Wisdom: The Seam and the Wine

'Could not that *Wisdome*, which first broacht the wine, / Have thicken'd it with definitions?' Herbert asks wistfully in 'Divinitie.' And with consider-able irony, he continues to make presumptuous additions to the sufficiency of God's own self-revelation, suggesting, 'And *jagg'd his seamlesse coat*, had that been fine, / With curious *questions and divisions*?' But the harassing interrogatives of stanza three are replaced by proverbial sentences in stanza five: '*Love God, and love your neighbour. Watch and pray.*' And the imperial mode of those 'dark instructions,' the sententiousness of those 'Gordian knots,' prepares the way for the brilliantly equivocal command of the poem's penultimate stanza: 'But he doth bid us *take* his bloud for wine.' *Take*, receive in the communion cup, *becomes one* with *take*, receive as a given. *Proverb* and *sentence*, not question, are the first idioms of Wisdom, and Wisdom is the image of the Son whose clarified and simplifying *rule* governs and predicates the *life* hid in flesh and time ('all the doctrine, which he taught and *gave*, / Was *cleare* as heav'n, from whence it came').

Proverbs, both 'outlandish' and Biblical, play an important part in the development and meaning of *The Temple*, in the organization of its concept of Wisdom, and in the emergence of its own self-reflective poetic theory.[1] 'The Church-porch' is, of course, highly proverbial in both style and content; and it sets up in nugget form many of the premises which will be explored in the lyric life of 'The Church,' torn, as it is, between the precepts and rules it *should* live by and its own inadequacies. 'All forrain wisdome doth amount to this,' Herbert states unambiguously in 'The Church-porch': '*To take all that is given*; whether wealth, / Or love, or *language*; nothing comes amisse: / A good digestion turneth all to health.' *Take all that is given* (of love or language) is, then, the natural law which prepares the way for the *rule* of

Christ in 'The Church': '*he doth bid us take his bloud for wine.*' And the proverb, as genre, becomes not just the beginning of Wisdom in law and commandment but the type of the Body's *rule* by the Head which is in heaven, and which is on earth as it is in heaven when its rule is 'copied' on earth. As it travels from 'The Church-porch' to 'The Church,' the imperative idiom of the proverb is transformed from disembodied precept ('Joyn hands with God to make a man to live') into the voice of the rule incarnate (as in 'Clasping of hands' – 'Yet to be thine, doth me restore'), of Christ himself in his Body, who, 'having put on Man, and *proposing a rule to us*, teaching us to live, and granting us to live,' figured at once both his own rule-will and ours.[2]

'Proverbs,' Francis Taylor argues of the genre in his commentary on the Biblical wisdom book, 'are most eminent ornaments of discourse, and excell in speech, *as kings in a kingdome.*'[3] Actuating the presence of the Man who is called in *The Temple* 'My God and King,' the proverb was considered to be a high-resonance literary form by those, like Taylor, who wrote about them in the seventeenth century: 'from them other sentences are derived by consequence, and therefore they *rule* over these latter, *like kings*, and other sentences must stand, or fall at their doome.'[4] Called 'Princes on earth,' '*ruling sentences,*' 'more excellent then other sentences,' proverbs lend to the language of 'The Church' the idiom of its Head in whom it enjoys its Being.[5] That idiom is Sentence, which 'doth *judge and sentence* / Worldly joyes *to be* a scourge: / For they all produce repentance, / And repentance is a purge.' As the proverbial '*foolish thing*' in 'Miserie,' man needs those Sentences of Wisdom as mnemonic re-collectors of his Being in the 'spring, whence all things flow': '*Man is but grasse, / He knows it, fill the glasse.*'

'In clothes, cheap handsomnesse doth bear the bell,' Herbert posits in 'The Church-porch,' couching his language theory in commercial metaphor: '*Wisedome's a trimmer thing then shop e're gave.*'[6] The 'trimness' and terseness of Wisdom and the proverb genre are the stylistic expression of its *rule*; and the literary character of its 'few words' become the rod which should, in the minds of most who write about the genre, govern life. The 'troubles of a mans life are from his tongue,' Michael Jermin reasons in his commentary on Proverbs, 'which are avoyded by taking care of our speaking.'[7] John Dod and Robert Cleaver argue similarly: 'the safety and happiness of the whole life dependeth of the well ordering of the tongue' – 'all our actions are sutable to our speeches, &. a good tongue is the means whereby they are well managed.'[8] Herbert's 'The Familie' is about such management and ordering: the 'Order' which 'plaies the soul' and 'Makes of wilde woods sweet walks and bowres' is 'Peace' and the 'Silence' of few words. 'Humble Obedience neare the doore doth stand, / *Expecting a command*' of proverbial rule without which there is a '*noise* of thoughts within my heart' and '*loud* complaints' as if 'there were no *rule* or eares.' Trimness, in few words, predicates the presence of Christ, '*For where thou dwellest all is neat.*'

As Herbert suggests by the title of his proverbial poem, 'Charms and *Knots*,' the terseness of the proverb creates the conditions for the proverb's obscurity. Profound and 'deepe sentences,' Cleaver calls them, 'and the more short they are, the more hard, and obscure they be.'[9] *Vox gravida*, '*A word great with childe*,' the vehicle of *infans*, the 'pro-verb' is understood by the Renaissance to be that which 'stands for' a word:[10] 'the word pro-verb,' Origen had commented previously, 'denotes that one thing is openly said, and another is inwardly meant.'[11] And the dynamics of the proverb work through 'the cleering of them by *interpretation*': 'it is the *understanding* of them by study that makes them to be profitable.' *Knots* are tied by the trimness of the universal rules obscured in 'darkness' of the sentence's subject – sometimes 'who' ('*Who* looks on ground with humble eyes, / Findes himself there, and seeks to rise'), and sometimes 'Man' ('at first Man was a treasure' but 'sinne hath fool'd him'). And that darkness is made light as the third becomes the first person, as the subject shifts and is made clear in the act of interpretation: '*My God, I mean my self.*' Universal makes contact with the particular, awaking its being in the 'quickness' of its sentence. 'I' becomes one with 'Who' as the word conceives its child, lending the experience of that One Man in whom we all *are* to each individual who would those '*Gordian knots* undo.' The subject-transcription of 'I' for 'Who,' (or 'Man' or 'he') is the 'copying' of eternity into time and heaven onto earth. Abstract precepts are given form, and *caveats* without persona ('When th'hair is sweet through pride or lust, / The powder doth forget the dust') are lent a local habitation and a name in the lust and dust which create the monuments of 'The Church.'

Proverbs 'Discipline' the Church with the precepts, rule, and presence of Christ: 'Not a word or look / I affect to own, / But by book, / And thy book alone.' And the 'rod' of that discipline works to silence the aberrations and individual deviations of *self* from the general rule. Every wise man is both a 'master' and a 'scholar,' Michael Jermin observes of that discipline, 'As a master hee sitteth in the chaire of his heart' but as a scholar he 'must hold his peace, *so that the lips may learne, they must be silent.*'[12] The wise in heart 'is wise *in eare* also, and heareth rather others than himself to speak. He heareth from others the *commandements* of wisedome, and so heareth, as that he *receiveth* them.'[13] The 'loud complaints' and the 'noise of thoughts' in Herbert's 'Familie' behave 'As if there were no rule or *eares*.' As Wisdom gains in strength over the course of the life of 'The Church,' she gradually drowns the individual 'wit' and individuating self-expression of the poet – 'As a floud the lower grounds.' The 'Wit, Art, Policy, Sciences,' impediments hindering 'the successe of the word, through the violence of selfe-liking, the sophismes of carnal reason,'[14] are made inoperative by the old age of 'The Church,' a Church grown into Wisdom: 'But must they have my brain? must they dispark / Those sparking notions, which therein were bred?'[15] Wisdom silences the 'dispute' of wit, eventually, as it does in 'Dialogue': *What, Child, is the ballance thine, / Thine the poise and measure?*' – 'Ah! no more: thou break'st my heart.' But most of *The Temple* is not about that silence, and its poetry is not dogma but representation of the difficulties in leading a life dogmatically, in the middle way. *Yet are we bid.*

The imperative idiom of Wisdom, '*he doth bid us take his bloud for wine,*' closes the 'seam' of definition. In the idiom of Wisdom, there is no need for the joining copula, 'is,' to sew together subject and predicate as in *this wine is blood.* The 'seamlesse' coat of the language of Wisdom imperatively commands the predicate into the subject, *two as one*, equivocally, as 'wine' is *made to be* both 'wine' and 'bloud.'[16] And the *rule* of Wisdom transcends the need of proposition, for it imposes propositions onto single things, without syntactical seams: 'So *this flower* doth judge and sentence / Worldly joyes to be a scourge.' An 'answer' can be in and 'contracted to a rose.' And the equivocal 'contraction' (a 'rose' is both 'joy' and 'scourge,' as a 'sonne' both 'light' and 'fruit') is an unspoken proposition which has been woven without seam into the coat of language as the type of self-communicating love which renders *givens.* The 'rod' of Wisdom's wrath and correction functions in the same way as the implied imperatives of love by commanding things *to be as one* logically ('Then let wrath remove; / Love will do the deed'): 'That which wrought on thee, / Brought thee low, / *Needs must work on me.*'

Wisdom imparts its being and predicates *to* the creation and *to* the creatures in dative equivocacy. Blood is the predicate *given* to wine equivocally. And the logic of 'Faith,' for Herbert, is structured by that given equivocacy, which *imputes a lustre to the creatures*, and renders 'them bright; / *And in this shew, what Christ hath done.*' Meaningless and obscure objects of this world reveal the light of predication by the logic of faith:

> That which before was *darkned clean*
> With bushie groves, pricking the lookers eie,
> Vanisht away, when Faith did change the scene:
> And then *appear'd a glorious skie.*

The logic of the affirmation of faith for Herbert is based on the equivocacy *given by Wisdom*, 'when mans sight was dimme.'[17] And Scripture, of course, is the repository of that given, predicating by equivocating one for all: 'Faith puts me there with him, who sweetly took / Our flesh and frailtie, death and danger' – 'Faith makes me any thing, or all / That I beleeve is in the sacred story.' The 'transcendent skie' of the divine has been *impressed* on earth where it need not be conceived but received as given, and this taking – '*take his bloud for wine*' – is faith: 'all the doctrine, which he *taught and gave*, / Was cleare as heav'n, from whence it came.'

Proverbs are only the beginning of Wisdom; Wisdom ends in Love. Without exception from Patristic through Renaissance times, the three Solomonic books of the Bible were interpreted as setting forth the progression of Wisdom, in three steps, toward the Truth which is to be found on earth. 'The *Proverbs* set out true Wisdome; *Ecclesiastes*, worldly Vanity; *Canticles*, heavenly Love. The first teacheth us how to live in the world. The second, how to wean us from the world. The third, how to rejoyce in the love of Christ,' Francis Taylor explains in his commentary on Proverbs.[18] And at greater length Origen had explained long before him that a person trains his natural intelligence in Proverbs so that by 'distinguishing the courses and natures of things' he may 'recognize the vanity of vanities that he must forsake, and the lasting and eternal things that he ought to pursue.'[19] –

And so from Proverbs he goes on to Ecclesiastes, who teaches, as we said, that visible and corporeal Things are fleeting and brittle; and surely once the seeker after wisdom has grasped that these things are so ... he will surely reach out for the things unseen and eternal which, with spiritual meaning verily but under *secret metaphors of love*, are taught in the Song of Songs.

Correcting man's originally distorted perception of the world, Proverbs teaches the first lesson of Wisdom by re-adjusting man's 'eye' for the world, preparing it for reading God's own unspoken metaphors for his Being. 'Who reade a chapter when they rise,' Herbert begins in 'Charms and Knots,' 'Shall ne're be troubled with *ill eyes*.' Accepting the rule of Wisdom as in 'Submission' ('But that thou art *my wisdome*, Lord') means that 'both mine eyes are thine,' and 'dispute' that '*I do resume my sight*, / And pilfring what I once did give, / Disseize thee of thy right.' When he accepts what God gave, in Wisdom and in the Sacrament received by the structure of faith, a man gives his eyes, and his commitment is changed from efficient to final causes. 'Now, if I do not give everything its *end*,[20] Herbert concludes in '*The Parsons Eye*,' 'I *abuse* the Creature, I am false to my reason which should guide me, I offend the supreme Judg, in perverting *the order which he hath set* both to things, and to reason.' And 'final causes' is the 'Schoole rule' which should be driven into 'the smallest actions of Life' – or else 'I am Covetous' by usurping the proper end. Until he reads the world through final causes, his 'growth,' subverted by irony, spells 'decay' ('When man grows staid and *wise*, / Getting a house and home ... / That dumbe inclosure maketh love / Unto the coffin, that attends his death'), for true Wisdom measures not from the beginning but the end – 'Since the last joy.'

The house which Wisdom builds (Proverbs 9:1) – 'as for him that wanteth understanding, she saith to him, Come eat of my bread and drink of the wine which I have mingled' (9:4–5) – is the 'Home' *which is the end*. The 'household stuffe' (as Taylor calls it), the furniture of that home, is metaphor ('Take away metaphors out of Scriptures, and ye take away a great part of the choycest *household stuffe* out of the house. God therein plays with us infants, and as it were stutters to us, and cures our eyes with clay').[21] The 'stuffe' of the poet too, metaphor contradicts its own nature, undoes itself, when it is received as an end unto itself, as wine *taken* for wine; and it undoes then the poet too, 'a foolish thing ... / *His house still burns, and yet he still doth sing.*' Entangled in the world of strife, the speaker reflects in 'Affliction (1)' on the false ends of his covetous abuse of would-be metaphor: 'I looked on thy *furniture so fine*, / And made it *fine to me*: / Thy glorious *household-stuffe* did me *entwine.*' For the 'fine to me' neglects the end of the metaphorical nature of the creation (fine to God) which results not in the 'flat delights' of tautology – and abuse of the grammar of metaphor (clay is clay, dust is dust, earth is earth) – but in the multidimensional equivocacy given by the axioms of the Cross ('The bloudie crosse of my deare Lord / *Is both my physick and my sword*'). The 'household stuffe' must furnish not only the house of terrestrial Egypt ('the house and the familie are thine') but the home in Canaan. What has been cryptically said in the Wisdom of the Creation is spelt out by poetry, transcribed from the language of God. What the 'copie' supplies are final predicates, the determination of a proposition of which men must be continually reminded: '*Then close again the seam,* / ... Call to minde thy dream,'

> An earthly globe,
> On whose meridian was engraven,
> *These seas are tears, and heav'n the haven.*

II ECCLESIASTES: VANITY AND THE PRESENT INDICATIVE

'Vanity of vanities, saith the Preacher, vanity of vanities; all is vanity' (Ecclesiastes 1:2). Herbert's 'Vanitie' poems are, of course, an Ecclesiastical expression of the perspective glass of the Preacher, viewing 'the very vanity, not of some, but of all worldly matters.'[22] The Book of Ecclesiastes, Donne informs us on the authority of Ambrose, is '*Bonum ad omnia magistrum*; A good Master to correct us in this world, a good Master to direct us to the next.'[23] The 'glittering vanity' and 'gloss of terrestial commodities' is in the rhetoric of Ecclesiastes subdued by the things that *are*, not 'shadows' but '*solide substance*, whereof the comfort, use, and injoyment will be permanently substantiall.'[24] Although Herbert does not sustain such declamation long, his 'Vanitie' poems invoke the idiom of the Solomonic preacher ('Poore man, thou searchest round / To finde out *death*, but missest *life* at hand') only to discover that it comes back on itself, as a Sermon to oneself ('Poore silly soul'). Caught defying his own imperatives ('in preaching to others' the Country Parson 'forgets not himself, but *is first a Sermon to himself, and then to others*'), Herbert first displaces the vanity of vanities and the *all* which is vanity onto other figures – the 'fleet Astronomer,' the 'nimble Diver,' and the 'subtil Chymic.' But 'Vanitie (ii)' traps him by the inevitable reflexiveness of sermon, and the 'vanity' theme comes home where it belongs. Herbert then becomes subject to his own rule, 'A *verse* may finde him, who a sermon flies, / And *turn delight into a sacrifice*': poetry itself becomes both sermon and sacrifice – 'Heark and beware, lest what you now do measure / And *write for sweet*, prove a most *sowre displeasure.*'

The divine science of his art is the area of potential expression of the vain which most concerns Herbert in 'The Church' – the glittering vanity which is *falsely written as sweet* and the '*false embroyderies*' which are preferred before '*solide work.*' All poetry, one might say, establishes new predicates for the world that is (love is a rose, absence is winter); but, religious poetry, as it should direct attention away from the world, from the 'gloss of terrestial commodities,' correcting in this world and directing to the next, establishes a new order of predication by writing for sweet *what is in heaven*. If it does not accomplish its job by predicating the *height of heaven on earth*, Herbert's own poetry, as he understands it, becomes subject to the Ecclesiastical charge, 'vanity of vanities.' Silly soul, Herbert addresses himself in 'Vanitie (ii),' 'whose hope and head *lies low*,' and whose '*flat* delights *on earth* do creep and grow': '*To whom the starres shine not so fair as eyes.*' The 'starres' of heaven and not the 'eyes' of this world are the proper *subjects* of the religious poet, and until he learns to predicate correctly that *stars are fair*, the poet after Herbert's standards gives improper priority to false shadows over the solid substance which is on high. He must render heaven as the subject of all 'sweet' predicates of earth. As the rule of Proverbs is to identify subject with subject equivocally, and to take *blood for wine*, the sermon of Ecclesiastes is a lesson in the hazards of falsely matched subject and predicate, for it is heaven and its 'starres' which are the fairest 'fair' and 'sweet.' By Herbert's rules for divine art, all predicates must be attributed to final rather than to efficient causes, or poetry, too, is the vanity 'which is done on earth.'

As it articulates the vanity of the present world and undoes the idiom of vanity which predicates earth of earth, the voice of the Preacher in 'The Church' relies heavily on the idioms and genres of memory to lift the eyes of the world away from present 'indicators' of earth: '*Call to minde thy dream*' – '*These seas are tears, and heav'n the haven.*' Lord, Herbert begins in 'The Sinner,' 'how I am all ague, when I seek / What I have treasur'd *in my memorie*': 'I finde there *quarries of pil'd vanities*, / But shreds of holinesse.' Neglect of the art of Real predication is both sin and non-being ('Sinne is *flat* opposite to th'Almighty, seeing / It wants the good of *vertue*, and of *being*'), and a life unilluminated by memory's perspective-removal from the time that seems to be (the time where the sun goes down and also rises) is a life which predicates the vanity and cobwebs through which we pass. God has decreed a different set of predicates than those to which we vainly subscribe by forgetting: '*There the circumference earth is, heavn' the centre.*' What Thomas Granger calls 'the vanitie of youth,'[25] forgetfulness, is overcome in Herbert's poetic practice of 'effectual' memory:

For youth being violently carried with headstrong passions and unbridled lusts, is apt to forget God, to despise instruction and hate correction. Remembrance is historicall, or *practicke and effectual* ... The latter is the understanding remembrance of that which *pertaineth to us to do*, or a dutie to be performed.

And the 'effectual' memory of Herbert's poetry inscribes the predications which were and will be onto things which 'are' evanescently in the otherwise vain flux of time.

Emblem, 'motto,' epigram, epigraph, and 'posie' are the genres of effectual memory recollecting itself from vanity: '*O write in brass*,' Herbert reminds himself of the nature of his task in 'Unkindnesse' – '*My God upon a tree / His bloud did spill / Onely to purchase my good-will.*' As it reminds, the motto condenses into the brass of solid stuff the prolixity of life which is loosely predicated in daily forgetfulness; and it inscribes what was, is, and will always be over that which 'is' but transiently. Man's prelapsarian self-predication had been a pointed *motto* – 'A ring, whose *posie* was, *My pleasure*' – and the mnemonic wisdom of Ecclesiastes, as it is heard in 'The Church,' re-establishes that pristine pithiness by inscribing 'The Posie' of art (condensed, undissipated by time) on the prolix substantives of this world:

> This on my ring,
> This by my picture, in my book I write:
> Whether I sing,
> *Or say, or dictate, this is my delight.*

Dramatized as 'Sinnes round,' the prolix 'adiunct of many words,' 'batologie,' and 'polylogie,' as they are called,[26] are the signs of a fool and the foolish man ('foolish thing') of 'Miserie' who prefers the 'dirt' he wallows in all night ('These *Preachers* make / His head to shoot and ake'). But for Herbert, whose duty it is to condense the world *as one*, such absence of verbal muscularity and evidence of thought distracted from the real is the stuff of sin: 'And so my sinnes ascend three stories high, / *As Babel grew*, before there were dissentions.'

The character of a Sermon is Holiness, Herbert remarks in 'The Parson preaching,' and that character is imparted by 'making *many Apostrophes* to God,' as, 'Oh Master, on whose errand I come, let me hold my peace, and doe thou speak thy selfe; for thou art Love, and when thou teachest, all are Scholers' –

Some such *irradiations* scatteringly in the Sermon, carry great holiness in them. The Prophets are admirable in this. So *Isa.* 64. *Oh that thou would'st rent the Heavens, that thou wouldst come down.*

The character of holiness, in apostrophe, invokes the presence of heaven on earth; and, '*My Master*' and '*My God,*' which bear no structural resemblance whatsoever to the usual syntax of predication, announce, nevertheless, the dynamic dispersal of all else by the Real. In the poetic language of 'The Church,' apostrophe functions as condensed and cryptic proposition – God is here and now ('By that I knew that thou wast in the grief'). Its energy created by the logical electricity of Relation, as in the Sacrament, the exclamatory cry is the *sign* of its answer, impelled by rhetorical decision ('let me hold my peace, and doe thou speak thy selfe').

Unconcerned with its own rhetoric, the idiom of Proverbs simply *rules* two as one, blood and wine. But the rhetoric of the Preacher needs to wonder what 'more doth win' and needs to command 'A strong regard and awe' – 'speech alone / Doth vanish like a flaring thing.' The Wisdom of Ecclesiastes, varying the Wisdom of Proverbs, combines 'Doctrine and life': 'colours and light, *in one.*' Equivocacy is here in the wise compression of *doctrine and life*. Apologetic rather than dogmatic, Wisdom's rule here is structured not by the givens of axiom but by the engraving stamp of the Head which is in heaven:

'thou dost *anneal in glasse* thy storie, / Making thy life to shine within.' Every preacher, 'partly the voyce of God, to wit in preaching; and partly the voyce of the people, in the act of praying,'[27] does *at once* 'bring down the graces of Gods spirit from heaven' and 'lead up the lives of men, to have conversation in heaven'[28] – 'And of that order of teaching,' Michael Jermin continues, 'let me note one thing from *Jacobs* ladder, of which it is said, he saw the Angels of God *ascending & descending* on it.' Brittle glass which measures time and otherwise pictures vanity is impressed with the solid 'storie' and mnemonic motto which rules eternity. Hi-story becomes one with the 'story' whose action is unrestricted by fixed verb tense. Condensing Wisdom into wit (the two-one wit of homonym and briefly stated apostrophic proposition), the idiom of the Preacher renders history persuasive in God's own accommodating deliberative rhetoric of *Example*, equivocating the one precept with its gracious effect in the lives of the multiplicity of history's individuals.

Like the 'Character' (a genre, by its very nature, equivocating 'life' and 'literary text' as in *The Country Parson: His Character*), 'Example' *makes one* of the 'Rule' of Wisdom and what it rules, embodying in the dust of time and human history the rule which itself remains unchanged and *constant.*[29] 'Constancie' is Herbert's 'Character' of the Preacher whose life is one with rigorous rule: 'This is the *Mark-man*,' Herbert claims equivocally (God's archer *and* an emblem to be marked) – 'safe and sure, / Who still is right, and prayes to be so still.'[30] Involved in the disintegrating mutability of the fallen world ('With sick folks, women, those whom passions sway'), he 'Allows for that, *and keeps his constant way.*' What is for always he relates to now, weighing 'the thing and the example' – 'What place and person calls for, he doth pay.' All made one by the equivocacy of his 'character's' generic logic, 'His words and works and fashion too / *All of a piece*,' his total being is the highway or ladder to God: 'all are *cleare* and *straight.*' As he is taught, he teaches-preaches too: 'To God, his neighbour, and himself most true.'

'The *sunne* to others writeth laws, / And *is their vertue*,' Herbert compares, distinguishing the constant Ecclesiastical man over the vain world: '*Vertue is his Sunne.*' The structure of his predication of what 'is' reverses the structure of Vanity's predication of what is not: syntax is the same, but subject and predicate are reversed. For 'the sun is virtue' is a different thing altogether from 'virtue is the sun.' The subject of the constant man, the alpha of his nominal order, is the end-omega of all things in God. Only the predicates are in the earth of creatures, and the thrust of his proposition, then, directs heaven, not earth, to earth. Constancy predicates the simplicity of Being in God – which is *life* – in the multiplicity of earth, equivocating wholeness of the parts, dispelling vanity. Stance and perspective are changed

in Wisdom: the humble and loving soul, Herbert characterizes in 'Lent,' lays
the burden on himself when doctrines disagree – he says, '*I am a scandall to
the Church, and not / The Church is so to me.*' Released from the limiting
perspective of self, where things appear to be to me, the speaker of Wisdom
employs linguistic structure which makes the whole Body of Christ, rather
than the individual part which is he, the end of the perceptual process; and he
is thereby freed into the Real and the point of view which is from eternity, an
eternity which exists above and through the vanity which now passes by.

III CANTICLES: THE GRAMMAR OF THE END

We should speak to God 'first as a beginner, in Proverbs,' Origen instructs of
the progression of Wisdom towards its end, 'then as advancing, in Ecclesiastes; and lastly as more perfect in the Song of Songs.'[31] In his commentary
on Ecclesiastes, Henry Lok explains similarly that Solomon 'who in his
Proverbs instructeth thee as a child, to a civill and honest life: in this worke,
instituteth thy manly thoughts to the inquisition of the highest good. To the
end, that by his last song of heavenly love, thy ripened thoughts might be
inflamed with that glorious bride Christ Jesus.'[32] William Gouge, along with
others in the seventeenth century and in centuries before, remarks that 'it is
termed a *Song of Songs* a Song that surpasseth all other songs. The Iewes (to
whom the *Oracles of God* were first committed) termed all the bookes of
Scripture holy: but this is the *holy of holies.*'[33] By Origen man's nourishment
in Wisdom is compared to the development from the milk-feeding of a child
to the meat-feeding of the mature, and Canticles is a banquet in the *meat* of
Love,[34] as is Herbert's final 'Love' poem – 'You must sit down, sayes Love,
and *taste my meat:* / So I did sit and eat.'

The Song looks forward to the end of time, to the marriage-union of the
Church in and as Christ and his Wisdom. 'In the meane time,' George
Gyffard observes of the Song, while the Church 'is a pilgrime upon earth,
there is (according to the ancient maner) a Love-song between them, which
King Salomon framed and penned.'[35] In the idiom of desire, the Song be-
speaks the 'Longing' of the Church for the heaven which is where Christ is.
'Out of this holy and Heavenly desire of her's, while she is on earth,' William
Guild writes,

yet having her heart on him and the desire of his love, and Love-tokens who is in
Heaven, we see what is the disposition of the godly, like *Jacobs, Gen. 32, Moses, Heb.
11, Davids, Psalm. 4.* or others. And how contrary the same is to the worldlings who
have their portion in this life.[36]

As a ring or 'token' of the promises of love, the Song prefigures another time, at the end, and the eschatological fulfilment of all the waiting of the Church: 'Who can read it with understanding,' Bishop Hall asks, '& not be transported from the world; from himselfe? and he be any other where, save in heaven, before his time?'[37] The book teaches, Bellarmine comments, 'a compendious way by the steps of creatures to ascend unto the Creator, and now on earth to be linked to him in love, that hereafter in heaven we may be united to him in glory.'[38]

A ladder between time and eternity, the Song of Songs is also almost always seen as a reconciling bridge between the spirit and the flesh. 'Let us note how marvellously God dealeth with us,' John Dove comments in the tradition of Augustine and Bernard, 'which to kindle in us the spirituall love of himselfe,': he –

stoopeth so low as to accommodate himself to the *fleshy termes and words of carnall love for us*, and by how much the more by speaking he is humbled, by so much we by understanding are exalted. Out of the outward words wee must gather the inward sense, and speaking of the body, we must be, as it were, out of the body.[39]

Bernard's own exegesis emphasizes still further the *carnality* of the Song and Christian love: 'that love of the heart is in a manner carnal, with which the heart of man is affected toward Christ *according to the flesh* and towards the actions which He did or commanded *while in the flesh*.'[40] Earth and flesh of the Body eternal displace the earth and flesh which runs but to dust and time, when Wisdom accommodates itself Incarnate in its final stage in Canticles, fulfilling itself as self-communicating Love.

'The Countrey Parson is full of Charity,' Herbert asserts of the virtue of the 'giving' communication which is Love, 'In brief, it is the *body of Religion, John 13:35.*' In the re-integrating effects of self-giving, another Body comes into being, a Body not without its own sensuality and warmth. 'Though private prayer be a brave designe,' Herbert qualifies in 'The Church-porch,' 'Yet publick hath more promises, *more love*: And *love's a weight to hearts, to eies a signe.*' The expressed community of public worship is an emblem of that Body created by Love, a Body which lends the light and heat of Wisdom to replace the dimness of mortal sight and the coldness of the world: 'let us move / Where it is warmest' – '*for where most pray, is heaven.*' In 'The World' Herbert tells the story of creative being, making a world through love in Wisdom: '*Love built a stately house.*' Simple allegory is fairly quickly dispatched by complex cross-reference between the allegory which is the creation of the world and its more concrete tropological meaning in the creation of the poem – 'spinning phansies' and 'fine cobwebs' support the frame of the poem and world, so '*Wisdome* quickly swept them all away.' Ecclesiastical Wisdom, preparing the way for Canticles, dispels the 'vanity' which has been built from false love, love-become-cupidinous, diverted from its end in God. But *Love* builds again, recreates the physical edifice and 'Home' of Wisdom both on earth and above: '*Love* and *Grace* took *Glorie* by the hand, / And built *a braver Palace then before.*'

'The World,' then, tells *at once* the story of Creation and poetic creation. Herbert's poetic world, too, born out of Wisdom, razes the image of the world which forgets God (neglecting his 'speaking' in it) in order to replace it with an embodiment of the ontological argument, referring all things to their being in God out of whose Love the world was made. Carnal experience in the flesh of lusty words, rich and lush, becomes the way of Love to and through the Wisdom of God – an 'ointment' (Canticles 1:3), metaphor 'drawn from that which is earthly, to make us in love with that which is heavenly.' God 'admonisheth us,' John Dove explains of the theology of the poetic principles at work in Proverbs,

and calleth us back by Parables and dark sentences, and secretly by things which are knowne unto us, bringeth us to the love of things which are unknowne, &c. *The mind by words of love which is beneath us, is stirred up to love which is above us.*[41]

Whereas the contribution of Proverbs to the poetics of Wisdom is the Sentence, and the contribution of Ecclesiastes the expostulation of living example in Apostrophe, the distinctive literary characteristic of the end of Wisdom is Epitome. 'The first Reason why this Song is more excellent then others,' John Cotton argues,

is, because this Song speaketh not onely of the chiefest matter, to wit, Christ and his Church; but also more largely then any of Davids Psalmes, and with *more store of more sweet and precious, exquisite and amiable Resemblances,* taken from the richest Jewels, the sweetest Spices, Gardens, Orchards, Vineyards, Winecellars, and the chiefest beauties of all the workes of God and Man.[42]

Epitome condenses and distils the vanity that is into a Promised Land and the enclosed garden of 'The Church,' the Body of Christ implanted in a place of meaning. 'Sunday,' which is the Epitome of the week, works by the logic of synecdoche to realize the wholeness of time and Being equivocally, '*Making the whole to stoup and bow,* / Till thy release appeare.' Whereas the 'other dayes' fill up 'the spare / And *hollow room* with *vanities,*' the model of précis and synopsis which is *given* in Sunday ('This day my Saviour rose, / And did *inclose* this light for his') is both a 'garden' (an ontological oasis in time) and a succinct gathering of jewels which will be the 'bracelet' of Solomon's Bride-Church at the end of time. More rich than the world itself, the poetic garden which epitomizes Creation on the model of Sunday displaces the 'hollow room' of daily insignificances with an icon of the *pleasure* which is to be found in Love recreating signs.

'Thy friend put in thy bosome: *wear his eies* / Still in thy heart, that he may see what's there.' In its final stage in Love, Wisdom accepts totally the vision of the world *given* by another who communicates that vision in sign through love. Prepared by the perspective realignments of the lessons of Proverbs and Ecclesiastes, the man instructed by the Wisdom of Canticles finds the eye of the beloved impressed on his heart.[43] His Lord, Herbert claims in 'Love unknown,' 'Lookt on a servant, *who did know his eye* / Better than you know me, or *(which is one)* / Then I myself.' Visual equivocacy of the eye-I is the final expression in language of a Wisdom *given* in Love. Presented with a series of signs in the narrative which follows in 'Love unknown,' the speaker learns through those eyes engraved with the seal of love in his heart the précis of condensed meaning which *marks the end* in its epitomizing emblems: 'your Master *shows to you* / More favour then you wot of. *Mark the end.*' '*All did but strive to mend, what you had marr'd*,' the sign-making eye abridges further, prophesying the ultimate in 'Love' known, when we will know even also as we are known: '*Who made the eye but I?*' – '*but I have marr'd them*' – 'And *know* you not, sayes Love, who bore the blame?' Last things are discovered as compendium, the distillation of temporally separated meaning in Being and its sign in time. Practice in the vision of the 'eye' of Love enables the 'eye' of the beholder, at the end of time and in its précis, to *become one* with the eye of the beheld, succinctly. There 'mending' is a complete transplanting of both vision and identity, of 'eye' and 'I,' when the Church discovers its final identity in/as Christ and gives over the eye-I which has so long detained it in the rambling periodic sentence of history.

Condensed meaning, the figure of the end, is the responsibility of the poet instructed by the Wisdom of Canticles to gather honey from roses. Like the Horatian bee who gathers and distils in labour, Herbert's poet must suck and express the extract of the best of time to make a presentable abridgment at the end. 'All things are busie; onely I / *Neither bring hony with bees*, / Nor flowres to make that,' Herbert complains in 'Employment (1).' The consequences are plain enough: '*I am no link in thy great chain.*' The ontological integrity of the universe is dependent on the 'Businesse' and 'Employment' of poetry and the 'sweets compacted' there in Epitome, contracting person, time, and place. 'The *measure* of our joyes is in this place, / The stuffe with thee,' Herbert explains of the logical function of the 'measure' of verse in marking and predicating the end by sign.

'It is conformity which makes, as it were, a *marriage* between the soul and the WORD,' Bernard expounds of the significance of the epithalamion of Canticles[44] –

when, being already like unto Him by its nature, it endeavours to show itself like unto Him by its will, and *loves Him as it is loved by Him*. And if this love is perfected, the soul is wedded to the WORD.

Importing the imagery of Canticles into his commentary on the Psalms, Augustine also speaks of the unity of the Head and Body, of which equivocacy is the type, as the meaning of the marriage at the end: 'He called Himself the Bridegroom, and the Bride ... If two in one flesh, why not too in one voice? Christ may therefore speak, because the Church speaks in Christ, and Christ in the Church.'[45] Active voice ('loves Him') *becomes one* with passive voice ('as it is loved by Him') in the grammar of the end when the Bride becomes one with her betrothed and is conformed to him. The subject who loves is conflated with the object who is loved. Thus, the speaker of Herbert's eschatological 'Love' poem, conformed to Christ's image as Christ 'bears' what he is 'lacking,' is gradually abstracted from himself as 'I' and recollected into himself as 'he' – 'You shall be he' – and the 'he' is itself an abstract totality of 'loving' and 'loved' ('Love'), a condensation of two-as-one, given new body in its resurrection, a new carnality into which the I-he participates: 'You must sit down, sayes Love, and *taste my meat*: / So I did sit and eat.'

As unusual things, appropriate to the end, happen in person, subject, and object in the final poem of 'The Church,' so peculiar things happen in the tense, voice, and mood of its action and equative verbs. Most striking of all the unexpected twists in 'Love (III)' is its use of the past tense to describe future events: 'Love bade me welcome: yet my soul drew back.' The use of the past tense to translate the future indicative of Old Testament prophecy was a commonplace of Renaissance Psalms exegesis: the tense 'said' that God's prophecies are as sure as done.[46] And many of the Psalms which bear the earmarks of the future indicative are seen more reasonably as being spoken in the optative mood.[47] Some of the enigmatic mysteriousness of Herbert's final 'Love' poem can be at least partially defined by the notion of an eschatological mood, neither subjunctive, optative, imperative, nor indicative alone (perhaps all four), combining future and past tense, active and passive voice, subject and object – ultimately more Real than the indicative vanity of what seems to be now. The mood here is an enhanced optative, grounding itself in and embodying itself as the carnality of desire and appetite whose completion is both the feast and the way to it, where he who eats is consumed as meat, in another and as the other – 'So I did sit and eat.'

'Me thinks delight should have / More skill in *musick*, and *keep better time*,' Herbert objects in 'The Glimpse': 'Thou com'st but now; wilt thou so soon depart, / And give me up to night?' *Better time* is in the 'measure' of Herbert's verse which plays a symphony of the Being which endures. 'Thy short abode and stay / Feeds not, but addes to the *desire of meat*,' Herbert complains further in the same poem, receiving the reply, '*A slender thread a gentle guest will tie.*' The proverbial reply is a terse prophecy of the eschatological dialogue in the last poem of 'The Church' – '*A guest*, I answered.' The brevity of the genres of Wisdom and the meteoric character of its Sentences, Apostrophe, and Epitome are 'The Glimpse' itself – in the 'eyes' of Love – anticipating the 'quickness' of the end and 'The Glance' of '*Thy full-ey'd love.*' Terseness is the figure of the totality in that '*one aspect of thine*' – 'When thou shalt look us out of pain.' Wisdom's syntax is such that it defies, by its conciseness, the distinctions between subject, predicate, and object, in the 'full aspect' of communicating Love, exploding, as it does and when it will, the vain boundaries and 'seams' of fallen thought.

IV 'FOR THY SAKE': REPREDICATION

This 'clause,' as Herbert calls it, '*for thy sake*,' is 'the famous stone / *That turneth all to gold.*' The phrase, which gives all back to God, is his 'tincture,' once *given* for man in loving sacrifice ('Weep not, deare friends, since I *for both* have wept / When all my tears were blood'). The gesture of the language of Canaan, '*for thy sake*,' by giving over, gives 'his perfection' in alchemical reaction, 'For that which God doth *touch* and own / Cannot for lesse be told.' By the simplicity and starkness of the 'for' construction God may be 'prepossest,' and by the tincture of the language which directs, communicates, and gives back to God, 'All may of thee partake.' Breaking up the word 'forsake,' the phrase 'for-thy-sake' imparts the end of the gesture of sacrificing love and puts the otherwise drab world into contact with its final cause: 'Who sweeps a room, as *for thy laws*, / Makes that and th'action *fine.*' Fineness is touch-contact with the end of all things in God now. Even the glass through which we see darkly now will grow 'bright and clean' with the tincture of the sacrificing preposition, and with it a man that looks on glass may 'through it pass, / And then the heav'n espie.' The 'sake' is the substantive end of 'seek,' and it is a 'finesse' of that seeking with the praise of God: 'And what I do in any thing, / To do it as *for thee.*'

As a hermetic spark or the fire of the 'flint' of 'Content,' the minute phrase *for thee* changes the chemistry of the physical universe, repredicating all as 'gold.' In the act of communicating itself, Love closes the seam of predication with the wine taken for blood; and equivocacy, then, by hermeneutic 'taking' of its costly *given* of Love, extends itself beyond its own verbal boundaries into things themselves and analogical simplicity which 'Cannot for lesse be told.' As the Wisdom of the Word once brought the world into being, so the wisdom of the language of the poet-priest re-consecrates it into Being, distilling the flowers of the unweeded garden of the world in a perfume which is 'sent' back again to God. The 'poore wreath' of verbal praise is *one* analogically and simply with the 'crown of praise' above only by virtue of the Love who communicates the 'give for' and the 'for give' of oneness: 'then shall I *give / For* this poore wreath, *give thee*, a crown of praise.'

'In praising might,' Herbert concludes in 'The Priesthood,' 'the *poore* do by *submission* / What *pride* by *opposition.*' Only by the humiliating abjection, subjection, and rejection of self are the praise of God and its re-integrating simplicity established in the lowness, meanness, and poverty of earth. Where there is humility, then there is Wisdom: the further he bends to the ground, the more the poet predicates the height of heaven. '*To put on the profound humility, and the exact temperance of our Lord Jesus*' is one of the requirements of 'The Parson's state of Life.' As Jacob's 'Motto' of humility, '*Lesse then the least of God's mercies*' (Genesis 32:10), was the motto of George Herbert's life,[48] it is 'The Posie' of his verse ('*Lesse then the least / Of all Gods mercies*, is my posie still'): a disclaiming of all merit predicates the presence and proclaims the 'merit' of God. '*The poor shall eat ... And they shall praise the Lord, who seek Him,*' Augustine paraphrases, introducing his commentary on Psalm 22:

The rich praise themselves; the poor praise the Lord. Why are they poor? Because they praise the Lord and seek the Lord. The Lord is the riches of the poor.[49]

Inverse proportion, not proper but *improper proportion*, is the tool of George Herbert's predication of the Wisdom of God: the more abject the vessel, the more exalted its freight – the '*poore* wreath' of praise predicates the 'crown,' and what is 'less' than the least predicates what is 'more.' *Exalt the poor*, Herbert commands with detached irony in 'Praise (I)' only to find himself apologetically one with that poverty in 'Praise (II)' – '*Small* it is, in this *poore* sort / To enroll thee' – and to discover, finally, the operative analogy of inverse proportion in 'Praise (III)': 'I have not lost one single tear: / But when mine eyes / Did weep to heav'n, they found a bottle there / (*As we have boxes for the poore*).' The glass 'was full and *more*,' Herbert continues in 'Praise (III),' after 'thou hadst slipt a drop / From thy right eye, / (Which there did hang *like streamers* neare the top / Of some *fair church*, to show the sore / And *bloudie battel* which thou once didst trie).' Improper proportion re-establishes the condition of the Incarnation: 'for He too, when He was here and bore our flesh,' Augustine observes, 'prayed; and *when He prayed, drops of blood streamed down from His whole Body*.'⁵⁰

The Parson 'setleth wavering minds,' Herbert writes, by diving 'unto the boundlesse Ocean of Gods Love, and the unspeakeable riches of his loving kindnesse.' With sinful creatures the Parson argues that God '*must much more love them*; because notwithstanding his infinite hate of sinne, his Love overcame that hate ... and this *as the more faulty in him, so the more glorious in God*.' Inverse proportion expressed in the paradigm, humility-Wisdom, gives shape to the Body of Christ whose Head is above and whose feet below, ruled by the Head, made one in Love, and a proper image of the Son. The drama manifested by George Herbert's predication of God is then not simply the one = One of analogous attribution but the two = One mystery concealed in the *gift* of homonym, making concord of the dissimilar. The blood which streams down the whole Body, then, closes the seam of what 'is' in the chirograph of the poem, and the 'trimness' of Wisdom there, once offered in the gross disproportion of God-made-man, makes of man a 'medley' redeemed by the *consonancy* of truth: 'He wears a stuffe whose thread is course and round, / But *trimm'd* with curious lace, / *And should take place* / *After the trimming*, not the stuffe and ground.'

5

One-Both and the Face of Anglicanism

I MAGDALENE: THE PLACE

'Shee never diverted towards the *Papist*, in undervaluing the *Scripture*; nor towards the *Separatist*, in undervaluing the *Church*.'[1] In his sermon in commemoration of Magdalene Herbert after her death in 1627, John Donne paints for us the portrait of a lady as the Anglican Church, defining the path of the 'middle way.' Even the manner of her dress, Donne informs us, 'never *sumptuous*, never *sordid*,' proclaimed the principle which directed her life: 'Her rule was *mediocrity*.' To begin my final remarks by mentioning that the *via media* discretion in fashion possessed by the mother of George Herbert is identical to the taste in attire demonstrated by Anglicanism ('Neither too mean, nor yet too gay') in Herbert's poem 'The British Church' is to begin with a very simple point. But attire is no simple metaphor in the poetry of the Renaissance, for the garment is poetry itself. Language, the stuff of the garment of poetry, is the sacred gift bequeathed him by his mother, Herbert tells us in *Memoriae Matris Sacrum*, his volume of Latin poetry which was printed together with Donne's funeral sermon in 1627. 'You taught me how to write,' he comments: 'That skill owes you praise.'[2] Her art of writing was her art of dressing. She did not indulge in the excesses of language and of ceremony, in the overdressing of the Roman Church: she did not spend the day in 'idle talk' ('language being chaos since / The time of Babel'). Nor did she 'Pile up her hair as high as pride,' Herbert further comments, 'but after doing up her hair / In a simple style,' she besieged the Lord with 'Sharp and fiery' prayer.[3] Her method in language presents to Herbert an idea of the middle way of the condition of language itself, its paradoxical reconciliation of extremes, 'this very *grace* of speech': 'Stern winsomeness,' 'wit / And wisdom mixed,' 'Thought and word exactly in accord.'[4]

By providing us with a parallel set of images for the Anglican Church in the literature about her life, Magdalene Herbert presents to the literary critic a key to the ontology of Herbert's poetry itself, to the locus and nature of the 'being' of a Herbert poem. My central text in all that follows here is a three-line passage from 'The British Church' which defines the 'place' from which George Herbert writes (the 'face' of the apologetics of Anglicanism):

> Beautie in thee takes up her place,
> And dates her letters from thy face,
>   When she doth write.

The Church, and specifically the Anglican Church, is the reconciling *place* of Herbert's both mortal and transcendent aesthetic. The human analogy, in turn, between the Church and an admirable but individual woman of seventeenth-century England finds its roots in a tradition which, once recognized, leads us to read Herbert's poem 'Marie Magdalene' more sensitively; it brings us to the heart of Herbert's hermeneutic and its dynamic equivocacy, which extends meaning vibrantly beyond the printed page. 'Place,' 'letters,' 'face,' central words in 'The British Church,' are also *topoi* current in the literature about Magdalene Herbert, and these *topoi* are the very substance of George Herbert's poetic, the very basis on which 'The Church' writes, 'When she doth write.'

In Magdalene Herbert, Donne finds a 'place' where Church and Scripture meet and are reconciled: 'the *rule*, for her particular understanding of the *Scripture*, was the *Church*.' It is such a 'place' that Herbert's poetry in 'The Church' defines and names ('Beautie in thee takes up her place'), for it is textured equivocally out of the tension of the middle way between the eternal precepts of Scripture and the limitations of the 'now' of the Church, and, thus, it is 'pinion'd with mortalitie.' 'And ev'n my verse,' Herbert complains in 'Home,' even his verse reflects the tortured reality that is his language itself: 'when by the ryme and reason / The word is, *Stay*, sayes ever, *Come*.' As the mirror of all experience, the language of 'The Church' resides in that homonymous middle territory between heaven and earth, a domain whose tensions pull between the precepts of Christ as imperative and the language of men which falls short in the present indicative. 'She unlinked / Regions linked: she took her joy / In earth's possessions, and in the stars,'[5] Herbert tells us of his mother. Her 'grace,' both personal and theological, provides for Herbert an idea of the atonement at the core of his religious language itself, an earthly 'vessel' which conveys God.

At the heart of the method and logic by which the life and person of

Magdalene Herbert became a *topos* for the Anglican Church (and, hence, Herbert's poetry) was her providential name, 'Magdalene' – 'Etimologie,' or 'notation,' was a legitimate basis for any *topos*.[6] In a letter written in 1607, according to Walton, Donne wrote to Magdalene Herbert, 'my not coming was excusable, because earnest business detein'd me; and my coming this day, is by the example of your St. *Mary Magdalen* who rose early upon *Sunday*, to seek that which she lov'd most; and so did I.'[7] At death, too, Donne remembers her name: 'her *Death-bed* was as quiet, as her *Grave*. To another *Magdalen*, *Christ* said upon earth, *Touch me not, for I am not ascended*,' but she has ascended now with him 'to his glory.' Both Donne and Andrewes focus on the image of Mary Magdalene at the empty sepulchre of Christ (John 20:11–17 and Matthew 28:6) for the duration of several Easter sermons on the Resurrection: 'come, see the *place* where the Lord lay,' '*Ecce locus*,' the trope begins, concluding, '*Non hic*,' 'He is not here, for he is risen, as he said.'[8] 'The summe of it is,' Andrewes summarizes in a sermon delivered on Easter, 1620, '1. The seeking *Christ* dead; 2. The finding *Him* alive.'[9] For Donne in an Easter sermon of 1630 the incident proclaims emblematically the news of a new 'place' for the Body of Christ, and his interpretation of that re-location is most helpful in leading us to an understanding of Herbert's statement in 'The British Church,' 'Beautie in thee takes up her place.' Donne puts an emblem-tag on the place where the Lord once lay, '*Surrexit*,' 'He is risen'; '*Non est hic*,' 'He is not here,' and that emblem is a preoccupation of his theology. It becomes his case against the Roman Church, the 'painted' and overdressed Church of the Herbert poem, which Donne accuses of maintaining the body of Christ in the place from which he rose, as well as his case against the Lutherans (Separatists), 'Ubiquetaries,' 'shie / Of dressing' in the Herbert poem, who lend God no special place. This '*For*,' Donne says, in '*for he is risen*' – 'this particle of argumentation' –

the Angel opposes prophetically, and by way of prevention, both against that heresie of Rome, That the body of Christ may be in divers places at once, by the way of Transubstantiation and against the dream of the Ubiquetaries, That the body of Christ must necessarily be in all places at once, by way of communication of the divine Nature.[10]

'Can we finde an *Ubi* for God? A place that is his place?,' Donne asks in an earlier sermon, 'Yes; And an Earth which is his earth' –

the Church, which is his Vineyard, is his *Ubi*, his place, his Center ... he returns to us here, as in his *Ubi*, as in his own place. And as he hath a place of his owne here, so he hath an Earth of his owne in this place. Our flesh is Earth ... he returnes to us in this place, as often as he maketh us partakers of his flesh, and his bloud, in the blessed Sacrament ... if to day I can heare his voyce, as God is returned to day to this place, as to his *Ubi*, as to his own place ... I am become his *Ubi*, his *place*.[11]

Not without meaning do we say even now that he is risen, Donne argues, '*Ecce locus*, Come and see the place': 'It is not nothing, certainly not meerely nothing, that God does so often direct us to frequent his Sanctuary, and his holy places.' But, he continues, 'this is farre, very very far from the superstitious fixing of God to the free-hold, which they have induced in the Roman Church, and upon which, they have super-induced their meritorious Pilgrimages to certaine places.'[12] Allocation of the proper 'place' for the meeting of man with God is, then, no small crisis in the mind of the seventeenth-century Anglican theologian. Herbert, too, finds 'place' a troubled theological problem; he sighs, seeks, faints, and dies in 'The Crosse' until 'I had some place, where I might sing.' And thus, it is no mean accomplishment to be able to say as he does in 'The British Church': 'Beautie in thee takes up her place.' For both Donne and Herbert, 'place' conflates with 'person' as the image of the Church itself is redefined by Anglican apologetics as not a dead but a living image. The traditional notion of the Church as 'Mother' is revitalized by the reality of Magdalene Herbert as 'Mother.' 'I joy, deare Mother,' Herbert begins exulting in 'The British Church,' 'when I view / Thy perfect lineaments.' And on his deathbed Herbert is said to have requested '*the Prayers of my Mother the Church of England*.'[13]

Magdalene Herbert's importance to both Donne and Herbert did not generate from the dynamics that structure cult but from the traditions of *topos* or 'place' of argument itself. Magdalene, the namesake of Magdalene Herbert, had been throughout the Middle Ages an image of the Church: her name, we are told, *magdalus*, signifies 'tower.'[14] And Odo of Cluny for one 'elaborates on the significance of the tower, explaining that *magdalus* or *tower* signifies the Church and that mystically "this blessed woman" Mary Magdalene herself signifies the Church.'[15] According to Helen Meredith Garth, Mary Magdalene 'was ranked with the Apostles by the Church and the *Acta Sanctorum* calls her the most Evangelic woman, the most fervent lover, the "*Apostle to the Apostles*," because she announced the Resurrection to them.'[16] Catherine of Siena, Johannes Smeaton observes in 1617, gave Magdalene the title of 'Mother' since 'the Catholike Church teacheth us all to do the like'; 'if we be in the Catholike Church,' he deduces, 'we must have the Blessed Magdalen for our Mother.'[17] For their own Mother the seventeenth-century Anglican Church chose a Magdalene of *Now*, Magdalene Herbert: other men 'Want her for their own mother,' Herbert tells us in *Memoriae Matris Sacrum*.[18] In the dedicatory sonnet of *La Corona*, 'To Mrs. Magdalene Herbert: of St. Mary Magdalen,' Donne informs the present with the Magdalene tradition of the past: 'Her of your name, whose fair inheritance / *Bethina* was, and jointure *Magdalo*.'[19] And still more important, he brings to the *Now* the central trope of the past: 'That she once knew, more than the Church did know, / The Resurrection.'

Herbert's poem 'Marie Magdalene' presents us with a series of paradoxes structured around the notion of Magdalene as 'example' and derived from an emblem of Magdalene at Christ's feet:

> When blessed Marie wip'd her Saviours *feet*,
> (Whose *precepts* she had trampled on before)
> And wore them for a jewell on her *head*,
>   *Shewing his steps should be the street,*
>   Wherein she thenceforth evermore
> With pensive humbleness would live and tread.

The otherwise lifeless words of precept *become one* with the otherwise sinful *now* in the dynamics of example and are made a living and moving reality of equivocal being, 'Shewing his *steps* should be the *street*.' In the reconciling *place*, which is Magdalene, the feet of the Head ('her Saviours feet') are united with the head of the feet: his precepts, 'a jewell on her head,' direct the course wherein she would 'live and tread.' In sacramental unity, the activity of the Head is embodied in the living present of Magdalene's life so that, as the figure of equivocacy itself, '*in washing one*' she washes '*both*.' Here is the type of Anglicanism, bridging the extremes of 'both' in 'one,' and here is an emblem of Herbert's poetic language in 'The Church.'

The figure of Magdalene in Herbert's poem is the *place* of the Church: 'she knew who did vouchsafe and deigne / To bear her filth, and that *her sinnes did dash / Ev'n God himself*.' But the place is a centrifugal centre of meaning which, in looser form, extends far beyond the condensation of the poem by the logic of *commonplace*. Magdalene is also 'The Church,' the place of Herbert's writing itself; she is the Mother Church of England whose gracious economy condenses 'both' into 'one'; she is the Mother, therefore and appropriately, who taught Herbert to write; and she is the figure of literary 'precept' equivocating itself – two become one – in living 'character' and example ('Shewing his steps would be the street'). She is a place which overcomes fixed place *in* fixed place: as one, she is both – 'in washing one, she washed both' – and, as an emblem of Christ's continuing ministry in his Church, she embodies his 'words' in 'works, and thoughts.'

As the both-one trope of Anglicanism is given in the figure of Magdalene-Church-Mother, the emblem of Herbert's poetic language itself, it pulls together the feet-life-journey of the poem before it ('The 23d Psalme') and the head-Christ-doctrine of the poem succeeding it ('Aaron'). Both the complexity of action ('Well may I walk, not fear') and the simplicity of the Word ('Christ is my onely head, / My *alone onely* heart and breast') are made one in the Sacrament which is 'The Church.' And it is the open-minded stance of Anglicanism, giving due consideration to *both*, which is the reconciling place which creates the accommodating dimensions of equivocacy. 'My God, what is a heart?' Herbert asks in 'Mattens' – 'Silver, or gold, or previous stone, / Or starre, or rainbow, or *a part / Of all these things, or all of them in one*?' All of them *in one* is the answer of Herbert's aesthetic in 'The Church' as it is the answer to his prayer in 'Mattens': 'Teach me thy love to know; / That this new light, which now I see, / May *both* the *work* and *workman* show.' At the centre of the paradigm of the both-one trope is the energy of logical Relation (work-workman), simplifying and integrating by relating place to place.

'*Letters*' are written from the face of the Church, we are told in 'The British Church': Beauty 'dates her *letters* from thy face, / When she doth write.' Letters, or epistles, are the major literary form in the New Testament, John Donne observes on several occasions. Generically, he says, Epistles are 'Relations of things past, for instruction of the present.' They err not much 'that call the whole new Testament Epistle,' he concedes,

For even the Gospells are *Evangelia*, good Messages, and that's proper to an Epistle ... An Epistle is *collocutio scripta*, saies Saint Ambrose, Though it be written far off, and sent, yet it is a Conference, and *seperatos copulat*, sayes hee; by this meanes wee overcome distances, we deceive absences, and wee are together even when wee are asunder: And therefore, in this kinde of conveying spirituall comfort to their friends, have the ancient Fathers been more exercised then in any other form, almost all of them have written Epistles.[20]

Letters (Epistles) in *The Temple*, poems written from the face of 'The Church,' bring together in one place and overcome the distances that range from heaven to earth: 'What have I left, that I should stay and grone? / The most of me to heav'n is fled.' Church bells are heard beyond the stars. Past events instruct by way of informing and forming the present of the poem: 'Yet Lord restore thine image, heare my call: / And though my hard heart scarce to

thee can grone, / Remember that thou once didst write in stone.' The letter of
the mediating language of Anglicanism is transformed from empty 'bodie,'
from the stone of Christ's sepulchre, into 'epistle' which can 'deceive distances' and convey 'spirituall comfort' by means of its equivocal destiny on
both the page and the heart in *one*.

The Apostles were 'frequent in Epistles,' Donne observes, 'And, as they
had the name of *Apostles*, from Letters, from Epistles, from Missives,'

so they executed the office of their Apostleship so too, by Writing, and by Preaching.
This succession in the Ministery of the Gospell did so too. Therefore it is said of S.
Chrysostome, Ubique praedicavit, quia ublique lectus, He preached every where,
because he was read every where ... In the first age of all, they scarce went any other
way, (for writing) but this, by Epistles. [21]

Language, Herbert tells us, was taught him by his mother. Her kind of
writing joined thought to word ('*Sententiae cum voce*'). Like a true Apostle
she preached everywhere: 'Letters, / Talked of everywhere, wing through the
world.' She is one of the 'blessed women,' as Donne calls them, who 'were all
made *Maries*, Messengers, Apostles to the Apostles ... (that is, Messengers of
the Resurrection).' [22] As such, Magdalene-Mother-Church-language is the
embodiment of apologetics and poetics at once, teaching that the words of a
poem and the British Church are but a face until they have rectified a heart and
equivocally given to it the face of 'The Church' as both-one. The 'place' which
Beauty 'takes up' and from which she dates her letter-epistles is the nexus of
the sacramental (where 'one' is 'both,' where 'wee are together even when wee
are asunder' for we follow one example). And yet it is but 'The Church' which
we see as one on the printed page.

The 'letter of the word' of language, the configuration or chirograph on the
printed page, the writing in stone, becomes one equivocally with the letter-
Epistle-Apostle who embodies the eternal precept in the 'now' of his own
example and becomes, thereby, the 'news' of the Resurrection. Far from
being insignificant, the written word is at once the one-both: it is the 'place' of
God and the place from which He has risen, the sacramental 'place' of the
Church – 'For the Sacrament extends as well to heaven, from which it fetches
grace, as to the table [language], from whence it delivers Bread and Wine.' [23]
Language is the medium of the Echo of Heaven in Now, Christ's dictates
in time, Scripture in the experience of the Church: language is itself the
via media, the middle way, and so Christ too had called himself the Way.
Language is properly, therefore, not 'dress' which covers Logos (indeed
Logos must be *discovered*), it is not clothing for the 'sun,' but the 'sonne'

itself. As the medium of the tradition (*traditio*) of God's self-disclosure, language is both the form and content of the revelation, as Herbert suggests in his poem 'The Sonne': 'I like our language ... / Who cannot dresse it well, want wit, not words.' Dress is the nature of the thing itself, for it turns upon itself 'in a sense most true,' and, in doing so, it becomes 'The Sonne.' Hearken ever to the voice of your Mother, the Church, Donne advises, 'quarrell not your mothers honor, nor her discretion: Despise not her person, nor her apparell.'[24] Proper dress, the trademark of Magdalene Herbert and the pride of the British Church, is no simple contingency; for the overdressing of the Roman Church puts Christ back in his sepulchre of the 'letter of the word,' and the underdressing of the Separatists creates no 'place' or 'face' for the Word.

   In the place, Magdalene, which is the commonplace of the Church, words are grouped together and brought together in an equivocacy which is absolute and ablative. 'Mother' – 'dearest Mother ... / The mean, thy praise and glorie is' – is 'Church,' 'Magdalene Herbert,' 'Marie Magdalene,' attached side by side (without connecting syntax), *in one*. Sin-tears-wash-feet, emblems of the original Mary Magdalene, are given one place together with the Church and its idiom of one-both and with the lexical set of particular concern to George Herbert: language-dress-Mother. All this in one word, 'Mother' – poetry, Church, equivocacy, sacramentality – condensed locatively, by virtue of the commonplace and its implied apposition: ablative equivocacy has no firmer basis than that of a 'place' shared in a word ('Mother' – Magdalene, Church; 'steps' – feet, street), and it is a fairly characteristic mark of the poetry of George Herbert.

II EQUIVOCACY: CONSONANCY, COLLATION, COLLOCATION

Linguists are just beginning to explore the lexical phenomenon of collocation: the theory of lexical probability that, given a word such as 'Church,' certain other words will appear together with it in high frequency, as 'altar,' 'cross,' 'windows,' 'music,' 'monuments.' At an elementary level, collocation can be explained by geography and the 'accident' of the occurrence of all the words in a given *place*.[25] But at a more theoretical level, where the context in which a word appears contributes to its meaning, the phenomenon of collocation should be an essential aspect of the study of the dynamics of poetic language, where the rules are not the same as they are in syntactically sutured prose. Magdalene-Church-Mother-dress-language are collocated, put in one place, in 'The Church'; and the total paradigm of collocations is the contextual

meaning of any one of the paradigm, as by the logic of synecdoche ('*a part /
Of all these things, or all of them in one?*').

It is with good reason that scholars of the Renaissance are notoriously
nervous about the introduction of modern terminology on material of
another age. But the area of investigation known now as collocation is not at
all unlike some aspects of the poetic theory we know the Renaissance to have
had, and neither is it at all unlike the hermeneutic theory which Herbert
records in both *The Country Parson* and 'The Church.' In his *The Garden of
Eloquence,* for instance, Henry Peacham describes with an illustration from
Psalm 68 what he calls '*Metonimia* of place': 'Somtime the *Metonimia* of place
signifieth the actions in a place. An example: For thy temples sake which is at
Jerusalem, Kings shall bring presents to Thee. Here by the Temple is understood the holy exercises and diuine worship used in the Temple.'[26] This
figure, Peacham continues, 'is of large and ample capacitie to contain matters
of great *signification,* and of many figures there are none more pleasant or
more *significant.*' More than metonymy, however, the whole practice of
topos, of commonplace, trains the Renaissance mind from the dawn of its
schooldays to collocate and to pull under one heading a whole structure of
meaning.

'Collate' is the word that Herbert uses to define the dynamics of language
which lifts its meaning beyond syntax – the 'judicious comparing of place
with place.' Technically, not identical to 'collocate' which assigns to two
things one place, 'collate' aligns place with place; but the 'lights combine ... /
This verse marks that, and both do make a motion / Unto a third' – and 'These
three make up some Christians destinie.' Escaping the limits of place, Herbert's 'collate' translates into equivocal both-one place,[27] and there it expresses the 'consonancy' of truth. That consonancy (which all Truth has to itself) is
dramatized in Herbert's poetry by the practice of homonym: *sound* is the
place which collocates the meaning which defies the limits of prose structure.
The sound of language is the holy place of 'The Church,' and its 'music' – 'if I
travell in your companie, / *You know the way to heavens doore.*'

In Herbert's poetry the hermeneutics of equivocacy match the hermeneutics which he gives to Scripture: place combines with place in the one-both
commonplace of homonym. The 'letter' on the collocated stone-sepulchre of
the page combines with the 'letter' of the spirit-apostle, living example, and
both are one. The Old is made one with the New, the icon is made one with its
meaning. Terrene place is brought into Relation with celestial place, as in the
Sacrament; 'Mother' is both earthly and divine, her 'letters' both 'sealed' and
'sent,'[28] and her 'dress' both a sign and the thing signed. The cement of
homonym is the 'cement' of the grounding 'floore' of 'The Church': 'the

sweet cement, which in one sure band / Ties the whole frame, is *Love* / And *Charitie.*'

Seven years before George Herbert wrote his mother of 'the vanity of those many Love-poems, that are daily writ and consecrated to *Venus*' ('so few are writ, that look towards *God* and *Heaven*'), Robert Southwell had written in the Dedicatory Epistle of his *Mary Magdalens Funerall Teares* that 'passion, and especially this of love, is in these dayes the chiefe commaunder of most mens actions, & the Idol to which both tongues and pennes doe sacrifice theyr ill bestowed labours.'[29] As too much of the best is evil, Southwell continues, 'and excesse in virtue vice: so passions let loose without limits, are imperfections, nothing being good that wanteth measure' –

neither too stormie nor too calme a minde giueth Vertue the first course, but a *middle temper* between them both, in which thè well ordered passions were wrought to prosecute, not suffered to pervert any vertuous indeuour. Such were the passions of this holie Saint, which were not guides to reason, but attendants uppon it, and commaunded by *such a love as could never exceede, because the thing loved was of infinite perfection.*

A place which makes of the middle way a feast, Mary Magdalene is excused by Southwell for her 'excess'; and that this notion is commonplace is confirmed by G. Markham's *Marie Magdalens Lamentations*, written a year before Southwell's, in 1601, where he derives the lesson 'that we should give way unto our woes, / *When the excesse no fault or errour showes.*'[30]

   The grief once displayed by Magdalene, her tears shed over the feet of her Lord, becomes the type of her sorrow for his death: 'And as in the spring of her felicity,' Southwell writes, 'she had washed his feete with her teares, bewayling unto him the death of her own soul: so nowe shee came in the depth of her miserie, to shedde them a fresh for the death of hys bodye.'[31] In the literature of Magdalene's tears, then, her life becomes the place which keeps alive the image of her Lord: 'if anything did make her willing to live, it was onely the unwillingness that his image should die with her,'[32] Southwell explains. As the figure of the future Church, she grows 'impatient of delayes' – 'She therefore ravished with his voyce, and impatient of delayes, taketh his talke out of his mouth,'[33] Southwell puts it, and Markham, 'Rapt with his voice, *impatient of delay, / Out of his mouth his talke I greedily take.*'[34]

   In her longing, in her impatience with delay, in her grief, Magdalene captures the tortured situation of 'The Church' as she desires to be with Christ but stays alive to keep alive his image. Part of this world and a-part from the world, at once, with him and not with him, at once: it is not just that Magdalene represents the Church to come but that she represents that Church in the condition of the middle way, midway between heaven and earth. Anglicanism's *via media* compromise, its delight with the both-one trope, is not just an apologetic stance but the stuff of the situation of 'The Church,' tortured between the extremes of the land in which it now resides, midway between the earthly Egypt and the heavenly Canaan. And her both-one is what she sustains of his image who once as both God and man consented to become one. Christ himself, as John Wilcoks comments, is *'factus Mediae Naturae*, a Mediator: Earth and Heaven had never met, but by his being exalted in *Medium locum*, the Crosse was between both, and Heaven there was content to stoop lowest, Earth being able to rise no higher.'[35]

As Magdalene stands in front of an empty sepulchre and later in front of her risen Lord, not yet ascended to the Father, her dilemma in apprehending and comprehending the image in front of her represents the difficulty of the Church to come. 'Thou wouldst have him alive, and yet thou weepest because thou doest not find him dead,' Southwell comments, introducing the problem of the now-whereness of God.[36] '*Quid ploras?*' Lancelot Andrewes asks in his 1620 Easter sermon, 'Is not *Christ* risen? Shall not He raise us with Him?'[37] For Donne the empty sepulchre becomes a symbol of the vacated *Ubi* of God, the shell that had once been the image of God in the body of Christ. Now, he argues, 'This Image is not in his body. ... We must necessarily complaine' that the Romans 'make Religion too bodily a thing.'[38] Drawing his argument from Jerome and Polinus, Donne questions further the inherent significance of 'place': 'How many men carry Sepulchres to the Sepulchre, when they carry themselves to Jerusalem?' –

Non Hierosolymis vixisse ... To have lived well at Jerusalem is praiseworthy, but not to have lived there. *Non audeo concludere*, I dare not shut up that God, whom the Heavens cannot containe, in a corner of the earth; and Jerusalem is but so. *Et de Britannia, & de Hierosolymis aequaliter patet aula coelestia*, Heaven is as neare England, (saies S. *Hierom*) as it is to Jerusalem.[39]

'I believed that Christ was risen, before I saw the empty Sepulchre,' Donne confesses, 'live Christianly, or thou art as far from Christ in the Sepulchre, and from all benefit of his Resurrection, as they that were hired to watch the Sepulchre, and to seale the Sepulchre to prevent the Resurrection, or as if he that lay in the Sepulchre had never dyed.'[40]

'Dishonor not God by an Image in worshipping it,' Donne admonishes of the external forms of the representations of God, 'and yet benefit thy selfe by it, in following it. There is no more danger out of a picture, then out of a history, if thou intend no more in either, then example.'[41] Magdalene Herbert's importance to Donne is that her life presents a proper image of God: not one to be worshipped (as an empty sepulchre) but one to be followed as example. 'Appeare to us, as thou didst appeare to us a moneth agoe; At least, appeare in thy *history*; Appeare in our *memory*,' Donne pleads in her memorial sermon: 'wee doe not invoke thee, as thou art a *Saint in Heaven.*' Enable us, Donne begins his funeral sermon, 'seriously to consider the value, the price of a *Soule*': 'It is precious, O *Lord*, because thine Image is stampt, and imprinted upon it.' To Donne's way of thinking, the '*nunc*' of history and memory is the proper domain for God's image: it must be engaged and sustained in time-present as rectifying example, 'when every one of us have lookt upon thee, by his owne *glasse*, and seene thee in his own *Interest* ... the *best example.*' If you will wake her, Donne concludes, 'wake her, and keepe her awake with an active imitation, of her *Morall*, and her *Holy vertues*. That so her *example* working upon you, and the number of *Gods Saints*, being the sooner, by this blessed *example*, fulfil'd wee may all meet.' Her body, like the body of Christ, 'being dead,' is still alive 'by having beene so *lively* an example' that it teaches others to be so to. 'Take so much of th' *example*, as of the name,' Donne wrote in 1607 'To Mrs. Magdalene Herbert: of St. Mary Magdalene,' at the beginning of his *La Corona* sonnets. For both Donne and Herbert, poetry resembles the Magdalene – it joins the words of the Head (precept) with the works of the Body in the present, 'purging us of old habits' (Donne maintains) and 'polishing' the heart, lifting us beyond its images,

Ut ipse videas faciam in corde, & alii videant cor in facie, That thou maist see thy face in thy heart, and the world may see thy heart in thy face; indeed, that to both, both heart and face may be all one: Thou shalt be a Looking-glass to thy selfe, and to others too.[42]

Magdalene 'did not mistake in taking *Him* for a *Gardener*,' Andrewes argues in his 1620 Easter sermon of Magdalene's encounter with the resurrected Christ, 'For, in a sense, and a good sense, *Christ* may be said to be a *Gardener*, and indeed is one.' He is the 'Gardener of Paradise,' and '*He* it is that gardens our soules too,'[43] Andrewes comments. A poem is 'a humble garden,' according to Herbert in his volume in the sacred memory of his mother; a poem is an imperfect image of the 'Eden' where his mother tills, 'dewy with those pleasures / That do not end.'[44] The garden of the poem is one in which Herbert imitates the now transcendent gardener in his mother

('It was / By you I come into the world; with you / To follow, I came unto the next'). She is the overseer of his husbandry, teaching him to transplant his posies from the book of Creatures, the garden of mortal things, now a speculchre ('the sterile world's mistake'), to the *Ubi, topos*, and 'place' of God. 'I have / A little garden too,' the poet claims, 'And closed to graceless feet its like / A posy budding forth a nest / Of sweet odors' –

> Here you shall be, and I,
> Every day on perfumes banqueted –
> The smells of many herbs. Just
> Wear your real face, one like
> The way I feel; do not listless
> Mix with my memory your face.[45]

As Christ is risen, Lancelot Andrewes reminds his 1620 congregation, so He shall raise us with Him: 'Is He not a *Gardener*, to make our bodies sowen, to grow again? ... the Head is already risen, the members shall in their due time follow Him.'[46] Christ is the gardener of the poet's images, making them grow again in the rectification of another heart and face, making them become another 'glass of God.' And so the doctrine implied by the encounter of Magdalene with Christ's *risen* image is at the core of the Anglican poetic of the 'lively' continuance of poetic images. 'I leave / The province of my flesh,' Herbert remarks in a Latin poem of the effect of the death of his mother which we come to recognize in his verse, 'with you / To follow.'[47]

Located in the middle way, 'The Church' stands as the logical *Relation* between heaven and earth. And that *Relation* is the core of the Anglican definition of the dynamics of the Sacrament: 'if our *Relation* be made from the *Signe* to *Christ*, the thing signified,' Cestren argues in his *Defence*, 'then, is the *Sacrament, objectum à quo significative: the Signe* moving us to that [*Sursum corda*] to lift up our mindes, from the earthly object of *Sense, Bread &c. to the body of Christ*, the spirituall object of faith, upon this Tribunal Seate in Heaven.'[48] Distinguishing the Anglican Sacramental compromise from Roman '*Idolatry*,' Cestren pursues the *Relation* doctrine, illustrating it with the usual gift-giver analogy:

our *relation* may be taken from *Christ*, to the *Sacrament*, as betweene a giver and his gift; and so, in *kneeling* downe, we take this holy Sacrament, as the *mysticall* pledge and seale of the body and bloud of *Christ*, and price of our Redemption, apprehended by faith.

Equivocal language is the *Medium locum* and the *Mediae Naturae* of 'The Church': 'In every Union of natural things,' Wilcoks writes in a sermon on the 'One Bread' of the Sacrament, *'vis unitiva*, some quality or other there must be, by which they agree in one, something *Mediae Naturae.*'[49] Homonym provides for Herbert the *'vis unitiva*' of the both-one middle way of 'The Church'; it is 'the *Relatum*, in which all the Correlates meet into one, *We being many are one Body.*'[50] Herbert's holy equivocacy, which is the 'dress' of 'The Church,' is the idea of the union created in love: 'the *Bond of perfection is love, Col. 3:14*,' Wilcoks continues in the same sermon on the 'One Bread,' 'and that is also one: it is called *Christs garment.*'[51]

'My searches are my *daily bread*; / Yet never *prove*,' Herbert complains in 'The Search.' But the search-way which is never proven is the logical position of 'The Church' in this world where she is granted only a sign-token-song of Love in the both-one homonym of heaven and earth. The *way* of Anglicanism is the Way which 'gives us breath,' it is the 'way' of the Sacrament which is the Feast itself, and it is the ladder-Logos to the heavens with the angels of God ascending and descending on it (John 1:51). '*Long Suffering*' is what is known of God from his relationship with the Magdalene, according to Herbert in a letter to Arthur Woodnoth: God-in-Christ is predicated by his distance from and patient waiting for his Bride, the Church. 'Thou tarriest, while I die,' Herbert complains in his own impatience in 'Longing': in Relation yet removed from the exalted God, he predicates the feet for which there is a Head ('My love, my sweetnesse heare! / By these thy feet, at which my heart / Lies all the yeare'), and he articulates the necessary and continuing discrepancy built into the life that is the Way – 'yet am I *stil'd*' (penned, written) 'Thy childe.'

'*We that are many, are one Body*,' Wilcoks continues along Pauline lines in the fifth of his sermons on the One Bread, 'a Body in the parts, in the union of the parts, in the Symmetry and Agreement of the parts, in the offices and Administrations of the parts; and *if we be of his body in earth, we shall be sure to be joyned to our head in Heaven.*'[52] Unity of the Body now, the wholeness of the parts on earth, predicates what will be the unity with the Head when the Body is conformed to the Head in heaven. Precept is the idiom of the Head, the rule to which the Church now falls short; but example, following after, on the way to the perfection of the precept, is the idiom of the Body, united in and as one example. 'By precepts we take our direction,' Andrewes observes in an illuminating sermon, 'but it is no less true, *Instruimur exemplis*, "We receive instruction, in a great part, from examples also." One serves for our rule, the other for our pattern; and we, as to obey the one so to *imitate* the other.'[53] Example structures the bond of love which makes one of the many parts of the Body: 'The Church,' like Magdalene, has trampled on God's precepts; but she shows the steps of his example to be the way-street, and she *imitates* the pattern when she cannot always obey the rule. The 'copie' of Herbert's chirograph and the 'imitate' of his art in 'The Church' is the gesture of the bond of love and a sign of the union of the Body in the one-both of his example, which is the way to the Head.

But Christ, as both the Feast and the Way to it, is found in the one-both unity of the Body which is on earth and which predicates the Head as it is in heaven. Example predicates the precept. And the physical bond of the external word in homonym affirms genuine analogy. 'My musick shall finde thee, and ev'ry string / Shall have his attribute to sing,' Herbert promises in 'The Thanksgiving' of the entelechy of his verse: 'That all together may accord in thee, / *And prove one God, one harmonie.*' Consonancy, concord, harmony, and homonymy are all there is to the 'proof' of the simplicity of God who is both-one, in the 'here below' of the flesh-dust of the external form of poetry and in the 'here above,' which are the 'two folds one.'

IV EPIPHANY: THE FACE OF GOD

Herbert writes in 'The British Church' that Beauty, who there takes up a place, 'dates her letters from thy *face.*' George Herbert's chirograph and its configuration of 'letters' on the page of his volume of poems comprises the 'face' of 'The Church' where we may behold 'as in a glass the glory of God' and be 'changed into the same image.' On that 'face,' then, the inner life of all the parts of that one Body are conformed to the image of the chirograph which becomes the both-one of the living and iconographic letter. The face of 'The Church' is itself the middle way between the stone-sepulchre on which was once written and all the parts of the Body throughout space and time who 'update' the letters as they relate to the face of those letters from which Beauty writes. 'The *face*' of the Church, Andrewes writes in his reply to Cardinal Perron, is the 'outward form of the Church' which 'is to be seen, as subject to the eye': 'In that is the *Face* of the Church; in outward acts, not in inward conceits.'[54] But in 'The Church' the inward form of the individual human heart is asked to conform itself to the outward form of the face of the both-one 'letter' which is continually re-dated in and as the reader who is willing to be made one in language of his Body. The 'face' of language in 'The Church' is no mirror which simply looks back on the reader redundantly, but it is a 'window' through which he can see himself joined as both-one to God, and it is the Way to God.

Like the Anglican Church, Magdalene Herbert, according to both Donne and Herbert, gives God a face: 'She was the purest law, / Beauty's vision to the world, the glass of God,' Herbert remarks after the death of his mother. A 'royal mother,' 'Her face for heaven fitted,' she lent to the present not a dead but a living image of the Gardener who presides over souls and poems, reminding those who seek him in the sepulchre of the earthly form of their 'powerful comfort': '*That he being risen for our justification*, we are also risen in him.'[55] You now observe, Herbert notes, 'the boundless / Beauty of her brilliant face / Was not mutable – was of the mind, / Not of the flesh.' This is her 'real face' ('one like / The way I feel').[56] It is 'the Image of the King of Kings' ('that Image in thy selfe'): 'And that's truly,' Donne observes, 'the *Ubi*, the place where this Image is.'[57] The function of Herbert's poetry is similar to the role of his Church and his mother Magdalene (the apostle to his Church) in giving God a place. For Herbert's poetry locates a face on the surface of language itself (the 'letter of the word,' the 'bodie' and the 'letters' of language) from which the Spirit of the body and the letters emanates.

It has been, John Donne observes, 'Gods abundant and overflowing goodness, ever to succor the infirmity of Man, with sensible and visible things; with the pillars in the Wilderness; with the Tabernacle after; and with the Temple and all the mysterious, and significative furniture thereof after all' –

The word of God is an infalible guide to thee, But God hath provided thee also visible, and manifest assistants, the Pillar his Church, and the Angels his Ministers in the Church ... This was *Jacobs nunc*; now, when he was returned, returned upon Gods Commandement; upon Gods Commandement pursued, and testified by Angels, and Angels visibly manifested.[58]

George Herbert's poetry, like the British Church itself and its living commonplace in the life of Magdalene Herbert, is the *nunc* which sacramentally embodies 'Gods Commandement,' his precept, his voice. The 'letters' of poetry are 'dated' (in time), 'When she doth write.' But the sacramentality of poetry can provide Simeon's Epiphany ('in his visible seeing of Christ'). Simeon, according to Donne, is a 'leading and exemplar' man whose letter-epistle-apostleship 'is assimilation too': that which Simeon had in his Epiphany 'is offered to us in this Epiphany, in this manifestation and application of Christ in the Sacrament; And that therefore every penitent, and devout, and reverent, and worthy receiver, hath had in that holy action his *Now*, there are all things accomplished to him, and his *For*, *his eyes have seen his salvation*; and so may be content, nay glad *to depart in peace*.'[59] 'My thoughts and joyes are all pakt up and gone,' Herbert complains frequently in his poetry. And so it is the justifiable complaint of a man who had seen in his poetry the 'face' of the temporal expression of his God. Ambrose changes the Antiphon in which we may join with Simeon, '*Nunc Dimittis,*' to '*Nunc dimitte,*' Donne observes –

and implyes not only a patience, and a contentednesse, but a desire, and an ambition that he might die; at least such an indifferency, and equanimity as *Israel* had, when he had seen *Joseph,* Now let me die, since I have seen thy face; after he had seen his face, the next face he desired to see, was the face of God.[60]

Her deathbed was without struggle or disorder, Donne writes of the *dimittis* of Magdalene Herbert: 'shee was joy'd to see that face, that Angels delight to looke upon, the face of her *Saviour,* that did not abhor the face of his fearfullest *Messenger,* Death' – 'Shee shew'd no feare of his face, in any change of her owne; but died without any change of *countenance,* or *posture.*' Her face, like the poetry of 'The Church' (the British Church), registers the meeting of time and eternity, echoing precept in 'now,' imperative in indicative, and marrying letter and spirit in example. Her face, like the face of Herbert's poetic language in 'The Church,' is the ontological 'touch' of the human and divine where heaven and earth meet and taste sweet in a liquor which is both blood and wine.

As the face of 'The Church,' language itself, brings down from heaven the ontological presence of the Being of God, so it takes up the beholder-reader-interpreter in the identity-modifying epistemological disclosure of the 'full-ey'd love' of God. George Herbert's apology emanates from the face of 'The Church,' justifying poetry, justifying the middle way of the British Church, and arguing the full extent of the Body of Christ whose apologetic motto, '*Lesse then the least,*' brings it down on its knees in recognition of and in testimony of that One-All which is the Real.

Afterword

According to the Gospel of John, Jesus answered Nicodemus saying that unless a man be born ἄνωθεν (again-from above), he cannot enter the Kingdom of God. There is no way the Greek word can be properly translated without the use of a hyphen. The poetic language of George Herbert is similar in its complexity under the smooth surface of simplicity. I have argued almost mathematically that the key to the richness and sacramentality of Herbert's language, as well as the key to his vision, is that one word equals two (a 'son' is 'light' and 'fruit') and that 'both' are 'one.' Simplicity, which represents the oneness of God, is reconciled to complexity, which expresses the distance between heaven and earth and heaven on earth. In arguing for my position about Herbert's language and the traditions behind it, I have created a mixed genre of theology-criticism, because after years of trying other methods I found that this method worked in explicating the poetry of George Herbert. Although I have no control over such matters, I would like to see Herbert criticism continue along these lines for a while (there is much more to be said), and to this end I have included a bibliography of exegetical and doctrinal materials I have used in my research, as an aid to future students and scholars of Herbert.

The subtlety of Herbert's language and thought forces the critic to adopt something of his own terse and epigrammatic style. To become too prosaic and single-minded obliterates not only the method but the meaning of the poetry. It is said of most introductions to critical books that they are generically defensive. In spite of many temptations to do so, I have tried to refrain from adopting a defensive stance with one exception: I have warned the reader inexperienced in Renaissance logic of the way in which it demands that we drop many of our everyday assumptions about meaning and that we develop a new way of finding meaning. This art is at the heart of Herbert' poetry because formal logic is at the centre of the dynamics of his poetry. To understand his poetry we must practise another form of the willing suspension of disbelief and enter a world where things mean differently.

I feel the genuine sorrow about letting this book go that Herbert felt in 'The Forerunners' ('Go birds of Spring'). For to work with the poetry of the man is to become, in one sense, the man (and a better man). And observing this at the end of a work like this is not a comment on the work, apart from the work itself: it is the ultimate point of critical statement here – we close the book not on a poem but on something more than a poem. When we close *The Temple*, we finish with participating both in the act of worship and the act of consecration.

It has taken some bravery to write this book, for literary history has not been kind to the pun and no secular history has been kind to the idea of equivocation. Holy equivocation, renaming all things and all the world into the name of God, is what we find in the poetry of Herbert. The idea of the chirograph as *both* the writing of poetry and the 'measure' of blood, the Sacramental area of *both* the sign and the thing signified, the Augustinian idea of *both* use and enjoyment, Wisdom's principle of the double sense of 'taking,' and Anglicanism's trope of '*both … and*' all tie together in the concept of *two as one*, which is the cornerstone for the poetics of *The Temple*.

In algebra we learn how $x = y$. In calculus we learn of the function of x. In studying the importance of logic to Herbert's poetry, I think we begin the calculus of Herbert criticism – more difficult, more sophisticated, but providing much more understanding. For my own part (as Milton would say), I feel that my ear has become much more sensitive to nuance (and, hence, meaning) in Herbert's poetry, and somehow, too, I feel closer to the altar at Bemerton and the remains that lie beneath the Chancel, both 'here below' and 'here above.'

NOTES BIBLIOGRAPHY INDEX

Notes

INTRODUCTION

1 All my Herbert quotation is from the standard F.E. Hutchinson edition of *The Works of George Herbert* (Oxford 1941).
2 Barbara K. Lewalski, 'Typology and Poetry: A Consideration of Herbert, Vaughan, and Marvell,' in *Illustrious Evidence* ed Earl Miner (Berkeley and Los Angeles: California 1973) 41–69. See also her 'Typological Symbolism and the "Progress of the Soul" in Seventeenth-Century Literature,' in *Literary Uses of Typology* ed Earl Miner (Princeton 1977) 79–114 (esp 89–95); and finally, her *Protestant Poetics and the Seventeenth-Century Lyric* (Princeton 1979).
3 Stanley Fish, *The Living Temple: George Herbert and Catechizing* (Berkeley and Los Angeles: California 1978) 66–7
4 J. Max Patrick, 'Critical Problems in Editing George Herbert's *The Temple*,' in *The Editor as Critic and the Critic as Editor* (Los Angeles: William Andrews Clark Memorial Library 1973) 3–24
5 Izaak Walton, *The Lives*, intro George Saintsbury (London: Oxford 1927) 308. Of course, the story itself may very well be apocryphal (as much of Walton is), but it makes a point which will be supported with other evidence from the text of *The Temple* itself.
6 Patrick Grant, *The Transformation of Sin* (Montreal: McGill-Queen's University Press 1974) 75
7 Margaret Bottrall, *George Herbert* (London: John Murray Ltd 1954) 3, 71–2
8 A.J. Festugière, *George Herbert: Poète Saint Anglican* (Paris: Sorbonne 1971) 140
9 Amy M. Charles, *A Life of George Herbert* (Ithaca: Cornell 1977) 51. See also p 44 ('it is likely that Mrs. Herbert, who took great care with her own hand, was the first teacher of penmanship for most of her children') in conjunction with my remarks about the centrality of his Mother to Herbert's concept of *writing*.

10 Sister Thekla, *George Herbert: Idea and Image* (Whitby, North Yorkshire 1974) 85
11 Richard E. Hughes, 'George Herbert and the Incarnation,' *Cithara* (1964) 22–32
12 Hughes, 23–4
13 C.A. Patrides, *The English Poetry of George Herbert* (London: Dent 1974) 17
14 M.M. Mahood, *Poetry and Humanism* (New York: Norton 1970) chapter two, p 29
15 Louis L. Martz, *The Poetry of Meditation* (New Haven: Yale 1954) 90–1, 302–3, and 319 especially
16 Malcolm Mackenzie Ross, *Poetry and Dogma: The Transformation of Eucharistic Symbols in Seventeenth-Century English Poetry* (New Brunswick: Rutgers University Press 1954) 181
17 Ross, 4
18 Ross, 178–81
19 Rosemond Tuve *A Reading of George Herbert* (Chicago 1952) 68
20 Tuve, 201
21 Patrides, 17
22 William Perkins, 'A Direction for the Government of the Tongue according to Gods word,' in *The Workes of that Famous and Worthy Minister of Christ in the University of Cambridge* (London 1635) vol 1, 440
23 John Boys, *An Exposition of Al the Principall Scriptures Used in our English Liturgie* (London 1610) 64
24 Joseph H. Summers, *George Herbert: His Religion and His Art* (Cambridge, Mass.: Harvard University Press 1954) 95
25 Summers, 189
26 Arnold Stein, *George Herbert's Lyrics* (Baltimore: Johns Hopkins Press 1968) 27
27 Coburn Freer, *Music for a King* (Baltimore: Johns Hopkins 1972) 156
28 Mark Taylor, *The Soul in Paraphrase: George Herbert's Poetics* (The Hague: Mouton 1974) 5, 14, 15
29 Stanley E. Fish, *Self-Consuming Artifacts* (Berkeley and Los Angeles: California 1972) chapter three, p 159
30 Fish, 157
31 Fish, 159
32 Helen Vendler, *The Poetry of George Herbert* (Cambridge, Mass.: Harvard University Press 1975) 220
33 Vendler, 224–7
34 Helen C. White, *The Metaphysical poets* (New York: Collier 1962 [1936]), 174
35 White, 175
36 Virginia R. Mollenkott, 'The Many and the One in George Herbert's "Providence,"' *CLAJ* 10 (1966) 34–41
37 Mary Ellen Rickey, *Utmost Art* (University of Kentucky Press 1966) chapter two, p 90

38 Rickey, 60

39 Judith Dundas, 'Levity and Grace: The Poetry of Sacred Wit,' *Yearbook of English Studies* 2 (1972) 93–102

40 M.M. Mahood, 'Something Understood: The Nature of Herbert's Wit,' In *Stratford-upon-Avon Studies* 11: *Metaphysical Poetry* ed Malcolm Bradbury and David Palmer (London 1969) 125–47

41 Aristotle, *The Categories* trans Harold P. Cook (Cambridge, Mass.: Harvard University Press – Loeb Classical Library 1938) 13

42 Rosemond Tuve, 'George Herbert and Caritas,' in *Essays by Rosemond Tuve* ed Thomas P. Roche (Princeton 1970) 167–206

43 James Ussher, *A Body of Divinitie, or the Sumne and Substance of Christian Religion* (London 1645) 31. There would be, of course, a problem with the date of Ussher's work if I were arguing that it is a 'source.' But I am not arguing for source. Both Ussher and Baxter, to whom I refer next, argue by the logic books that were commonly read in that day, and they, thus, give us a picture of the way in which theologians were absorbing the material in those books.

44 Ussher, 31. I have taken the liberty here and throughout my text of italicizing material when I see fit: when either a / the material is very much to the point, or b / a word (or phrase) of Herbert text has established 'loaded' meaning.

45 Ussher, 32. As we know, Renaissance oratory paid a considerable amount of respect to the *audience* toward which its argument was directed. This is one thing that makes a final decision about the 'high' and 'low' Anglicanism of a given author a difficult one: Ussher spoke from the midst of a Catholic territory (Ireland) and tended to stress the reforms. This makes his Anglicanism appear 'low,' for instance, but I hardly think that this is, finally, the case. The absence of such a consideration, of *to whom and under what circumstances* a statement in seventeenth-century apologetics is made, is one thing that trips up Malcolm Ross to the extent that he can be led to believe that even Laud was, finally, essentially 'Protestant' (Ross, 62).

46 Richard Baxter, *Certain Disputations of Right to Sacraments and the True Nature of Visible Christianity* (London 1658) 427–8. Baxter is, of course, classified usually as a 'Puritan' divine because of his attitudes toward Church government. But the more one reads of him, the more one realizes that he is committed to the idea of a 'Catholic' Church, a fact which becomes most obvious in his *Catholic Communion* arguments with John Owen. Dogmatically, then, Baxter makes many statements that resemble what we can best describe as 'the middle way.' A much more precise definition of the what and where of Herbert's own Anglicanism will be developed throughout my text.

47 Baxter, 474

48 Edward Leigh, *Critica Sacra: or, Philologicall and Theologicall Observations* (London 1639) 239

49 Herbert Thorndike, *Of the Principles of Christian Truth* (1659), in *Theological Works*, vol 2 (Oxford 1845) 567

50 Thorndike, 275–7

51 Lancelot Andrewes, *A Pattern of Catechistical Doctrine* (1630), in *Works* (Oxford 1841) 58–9

52 The meaning of the *breaking* the bread is equated with the *sacrifice* of Christ in seventeenth-century Anglican theology. As I read it, Herbert's *breaking* of the letter (as in 'Paradise') is a renewal of that Sacrifice once made on the Cross at the beginning of 'The Church': *Logos* is broken in order to mend.

53 'George Herbert and Caritas,' 174

54 St Augustine, *On Christian Doctrine* trans D. W. Robertson, Jr (New York: The Liberal Arts Press 1958) 14–15

55 *Categories*, 37

56 All references to the Latin poetry I render in the translation of Mark McCloskey and Paul R. Murphy (Athens: Ohio University Press 1965). This quotation appears in the second poem of *Memoriae Matris Sacrum* (McCloskey and Murphy, 125).

57 Most of my statements in this paragraph about the nature of the cases of nouns, and all of my quotations, are from Mason Hammond's *Latin: A Historical and Linguistic Handbook* (Cambridge, Mass.: Harvard University Press 1976) 146–65. My reasons for choosing *Latin* grammar are obvious: it is the grammar which was first taught and by whose schemes English grammar was interpreted in the seventeenth century.

58 See for instance, my 'John Donne and the Grammar of Redemption,' *ESC* 5 (1979) 125–39. It should be noted that I at this point depart, as much as possible, from the idiom of attribution, that is, putting my own statements in the historical framework of the scholarship of others. My reasons for this are simply practical: there is a great deal of background here, and it is a sin against Herbert's poetry to make it cumbersome (for this reason I have also included a bibliography rather than try to suggest the breadth of the materials used here in these notes). It is with great poignancy that I recall the words of Rosemond Tuve in her *Reading* of George Herbert: 'Too much "learning." Too many footnotes required. There is no answer to this. It is a long road. All the same I do not know why we should not walk in it. Who are we, that our time is too short to understand George Herbert?' (p 99)

CHAPTER ONE

1 Here, again, is the 'measure' pun in conjunction with the idea of *writing*: to 'measure' is *both* to quantify/qualify and to versify.

2 In chapter five I will speak of Herbert's collocation of the idea of *writing* with the

figures of both the Church and his Mother, Magdalene Herbert. In the meantime, it is interesting to see that even Herbert's early poems reveal a preoccupation with the concept of the chirograph and its relation to poetic theory. And one does well to remember that it was indeed Magdalene Herbert who, quite literally, taught him chirography.

3 See Robert J. Clements, *Picta Poesis* (Rome 1960) 135.

4 Cassiodorus, *An Introduction to Divine and Human Readings* trans Leslie Webber Jones (New York: Columbia University Press 1946) 35

5 N. Byfield, *An Exposition upon the Epistle to the Colossians* (London 1617) 66

6 *A Commentarie of M. John Calvin upon the Epistle to the Colosians* trans R.V. (London 1581) 47–8

7 Lancelot Ridley, *An Exposicion in Englishe upon the Epistle of S. Paule to the Colossians* (London 1548)

8 This issue will be discussed at length in chapter three where I will examine Herbert's attitudes toward other ceremonies (kneeling, for instance) beyond the idea of the *handwriting which Christ nailed to the Cross.*

9 See his notes 'To the 94 Consid.' of Valdesso in Hutchinson, 319–20. *The Sermons of John Donne* ed G.F. Potter and Evelyn Simpson, 10 vols (Berkeley and Los Angeles: California 1953–62) vol 8, 347.

10 *The Sermons of John Donne* ed G.F. Potter and Evelyn Simpson, 10 vols (Berkeley and Los Angeles: California 1953–62) vol 8, 347

11 *Sermons,* vol 10, 196

12 E.D. Hirsch, Jr, *Validity in Interpretation* (New Haven and London: Yale 1966) 78–89

13 David Dickson, *An Exposition of All St. Pauls Epistles* (London 1659) 75 (commentary on 2 Corinthians 3: 1–8)

14 My reading of this poem overlaps, somewhat, with that offered by Stanley Fish in *The Living Temple.* My points of difference are the following: a / that Fish limits himself to only one-half of the Anglican compromise; b / that what is true for this poem about the relation of the letter and the spirit is not true for all poems in *The Temple.* The 'letter' gains status in *The Temple* as meaningful icon: this becomes clear in 'The British Church.'

15 Augustine, *Commentary on the Psalms,* in *A Library of Fathers,* 6 vols (Oxford 1947) vol 1, 62 (commentary on Psalm 8)

16 *Sermons,* vol 6, 223

17 Francis Bacon, *Advancement of Learning* (2, chap 13) in *Advancement of Learning and Novum Organum* (New York: Wiley 1944) 70

18 Sermons, vol 6, 223

19 *The Homilies of S. John Chrysostom ... on the Second Epistle of St. Paul ... to the Corinthians,* in *A Library of Fathers* vol 21 (Oxford 1848) 89–90

20 *Categories,* 45

21 *Sermons,* vol 9, 77
22 *Sermons,* vol 5, 368
23 Ibid
24 *The Complete Poetry of Richard Crashaw* intro and ed George Walton Williams (New York: Anchor 1970) 68
25 Richard Baxter, *Poetical Fragments: Heart-Imployment with God and Itself* (London 1681), 'To the Reader'
26 Ibid
27 Henry King, *David's Enlargement* (Oxford 1625) 4–5
28 George Hakewill, *King David's Vow for Reformation of Himself* (London 1621) 1
29 *Sermons,* vol 6, 49
30 Augustine, *De Trinitate* bk 8. Also see Louis Martz, *The Poetry of Meditation,* 35–6.
31 It has long been my suspicion that Herbert, while at Cambridge, may have been more of a Puritan than he is in the final form of *The Temple.* In his 1620 letter to his sister, 'Think not my silence forgetfulness,' for instance, Herbert writes, 'though businesses may stop my hand, yet my heart, a much better member, is alwayes with you' (Hutchinson, 371). The fact that there is an entirely different version of 'Trinitie Sunday' in the Williams MS would suggest the lateness of the poem in *The Temple.*
32 The image that Amy Charles gives us of Herbert crossing the road at Bemerton to sing his poems to the accompaniment of his lute in Church would suggest that a very real connection existed in Herbert's mind between the activities of heart, mouth, and hand. This is no 'metaphysical conceit' but a serious consideration in the meaning of poetry as worship: the mouth also took part.
33 All my terms here are the very useful terms of John Macquarrie in *Principles of Christian Theology* (New York: Scribners 1966).
34 See Luke, chapter 1: 'Forasmuch as many have taken *in hand* to set forth in order a declaration of those things which are most surely believed among us ... It seemed good to me also, having had a perfect understanding of all things from the very first, *to write unto thee in order,* most excellent Theophilus.'
35 John Bulwer, *Chirologia: or the Naturall Language of the Hand* (London 1644) 142–3
36 Cassiodorus, 133
37 Bulwer, 2–3
38 *Sermons,* vol 8, 342–3
39 Lancelot Andrewes, *Ninety-Six Sermons* vol 2 (Oxford 1841) 30–1
40 Richard Baxter, together with some modern theologians, argues strenuously from the logic books that all analogy of proper proportion is a form of equivocation.
41 Theologians are quick to demonstrate that whereas 'being' and substance-essence

are separate in the creatures, Being *is* the substance-essence of God. Thus, Herbert would appear to 'pare' substance (as he elsewhere 'pares' language) down to pure being-substance, in 'one advise.'

CHAPTER TWO

1 Part of my argument here was anticipated by my 1969 article in *ELH*, 'The Voice of George Herbert's "The Church,"' the substance of which has since been absorbed and taken for granted by a great deal of Herbert criticism. My apologies to those whose reading of that article has been hindered by my then deeming it unnecessary to translate the Latin. The emphasis here is different and is finally, I think, where it should be: not on the Psalms themselves but on the Church.

2 Paul's eucharistic texts are of great importance in understanding this concept. See 1 Corinthians 10:16–17; 1 Corinthians 11:23–7; 1 Corinthians 12:11–27; as well as all the other *one man* texts sprinkled throughout the letters of Paul.

3 John Jewell, *A Treatise of Holie Scriptures* (1570) in *The Works* (London 1609) 215

4 Michael Jermin, *Paraphrastical Meditations ... Commentarie upon the Whole Booke of the Proverbs of Solomon* (London 1638) 325–6

5 William Perkins, 'The Art of Prophecying,' trans Thomas Tuke, in *The Workes* (London 1635) 2 vols; vol 2, 659, 656

6 St Augustine, *Enarratio in Psalmos* (*Pat. Lat.*, vols 36–7). The translation used throughout is in *A Library of Fathers* (Oxford 1847) 6 vols. This passage is from the commentary on Psalm 43 and is to be found in the Oxford translation, vol 2, 198–9.

7 *Psalms Commentary*, vol 3, 522 (Psalm 75)

8 *Psalms Commentary*, vol 1, 144 (Psalm 22)

9 Ibid

10 *Psalms Commentary*, vol 2, 210 (Psalm 44)

11 Ibid

12 *Psalms Commentary*, vol 6, 220 (Psalm 140)

13 *Psalms Commentary*, vol 1, 238 (Psalm 31)

14 *Psalms Commentary*, vol 4, 189 (Psalm 86)

15 *The Writings of Irenaeus* trans Alexander Roberts and W.H. Rambaut (Edinburgh 1868) vol 1

16 John Jewell, *A Treatise of the Sacraments*, in *The Works*, 275

17 James Ussher, *The Substance of that which was delivered in a Sermon Before the Commons House of Parliament, in St. Margarets Church at Westminister, the 18. of February, 1620* (London 1621) 21

18 *The Correspondence of John Cosin* (London 1869) 238

19 William Nicolson, *A Plain but Full Exposition of the Catechism of the Church of England* (London 1662) 166

20 James Ussher, *A Body of Divinitie*, 407
21 James Ussher, *Immanuel, or the Mystery of the Incarnation of the Son of God* (London 1638) 53
22 James Ussher, *Sermon Before the Commons House*, 13
23 William Nicolson, *Exposition of the Catechism*, 193
24 John Cosin, *Correspondence*, 262
25 John Wilcoks, *Six Sermons* (London 1641) 29–30
26 John Wilcoks, *Six Sermons*, 37
27 The notion can be found throughout the Psalms Commentaries of Augustine and Jerome, for a start. See also, for instance, John Day, *Day's Descant on Davids Psalmes* (Oxford 1620) 24; and Henry King, *David's Enlargement* (Oxford 1625) 2–3.
28 John Wilcoks, *Six Sermons*, 36
29 John Wilcoks, *Six Sermons*, 40
30 There is more about synecdoche, because of its important connection with Augustinianism, in the next chapter. In order to keep the records straight, I think it is well to record the displeasure of a Roman Catholic named Radford who complained in 1605 about the verbal emphasis in such explanations: 'When *Tertullian* and *S. Augustine* say Christ gave a figure or signe of his body, the *Protestant Grammarians* understand a Rhetoricall figure as *Metonymia* or *Synechdoche*, or such a figure as set up at an Alehouse or Wine-taverne ... Signes and figures in the Sacraments consist of words and the matter' (*A Directorie Teaching the Way to the Truth*, 215).
31 James Ussher, *Sermon Before the Commons House*, 16
32 James Ussher, *Sermon Before the Commons House*, 14–15
33 Ibid
34 Henry Ainsworth, *Annotations Upon the Five Bookes of Moses, the Booke of Psalmes, and the Song of Songs, Canticles* (London 1627) 127–8
35 *Psalms Commentary* vol 5, 326 (Psalm 9).
36 James Ussher, *A Body of Divinitie*, 31–2
37 See the standard seventeenth-century Anglican exegesis of the 23rd Psalm by Thomas Jackson, *Davids Pastorall Poeme: or Sheepheards Song* (London 1603); and Samuel Smith, *The Chiefe Shepheard: or, An Exposition upon ye xxiii Psalme* (London 1625). Herbert seems really indebted to Jackson in his own version of the Psalm.

CHAPTER THREE

1 There is, however, reference to George Herbert's debt to Augustine's (and Cicero's) *uti-frui* concept in Rosemond Tuve's 'George Herbert and Caritas,' 201–6. But Tuve does not connect the theme with this poem.

2 St Augustine, *On Christian Doctrine* trans D.W. Robertson, Jr (New York: The Liberal Arts Press 1958) 9–10 (bk 1, chap 3)
3 Ibid, 10 (bk 1, chap 5)
4 Ibid, 10 (bk 1, chap 4)
5 Donne, *Sermons*, vol 10, 196
6 *Confessions* trans J.G. Pilkington (Edinburgh 1876), in *Works*, vol 14, 272 (bk 10, chap 33)
7 *On Christian Doctrine*, 10 (bk 1, chap 4)
8 See Herbert's explicit use of the Ulysses figure in poem xi of *Memoriae Matris Sacrum* ('Dum librata suis haeret ...'): 'So here and there I go about, / And should by right be called another / Ulysses; let this death of yours as well / Be to me another Iliad' (trans Mark McCloskey and Paul R. Murphy, *The Latin Poetry of George Herbert* Ohio University Press 1965). It is interesting that the wanderer-Ulysses figure appears frequently in the language theory which emerges from the commentaries on the Wisdom books of the Bible and the Psalms in the seventeenth century. See Michael Jermin, *Paraphrastical Meditations*, 2; and Thomas Gataker, *David's Instructer* (London 1620) 14–15.
9 *On Christian Doctrine*, 88–9
10 As I have said in another context, the persona at the beginning of 'The Church' has a different relationship with the author from that of the persona at the end of 'The Church.' The external form of the poem is gradually accepted as it is reconciled to and made one with living meaning.
11 St Augustine, *The Trinity* trans Stephen McKenna (Washington, D.C.: Catholic University of America Press 1963) 304–5 (bk 10, chap 7)
12 Ibid
13 William Austin, *Devotionis Augustinianae Flamma* (London 1635) 2
14 St Augustine, *On the Trinity* ed Marcus Dods (Edinburgh 1873), in *Works*, vol 7, 178
15 Ibid, 177
16 Austin, *Devotionis*, 14. The ladder, Jacob's ladder, appears throughout the literature of the followers of Augustine: St Bonaventure, *Itinerarium Mentis in Deum*, *The Franciscan Vision* trans Father James (London 1937) 18; Bellarmine, *The Ascent of the Mind to God by a Ladder of Things Created* trans T.B. (London 1928) xvii, xxi–xxii. The traffic between heaven and earth is an image deeply implanted in Herbert's concept of poetry.
17 William Laud, *A Relation of the Conference between William Laud ... And Mr. Fisher* (London 1639), Dedication to Charles
18 John Cosin, *Notes on the Book of Common Prayer*, in *Works* vol 5 (Oxford 1855) 14
19 Cosin, *Notes*, 344–5
20 William Laud, *Speech Delivered in the Star-Chamber* (London 1637) 51

21 Thomas Cestren, *Defence of the Innocencie of the Three Ceremonies of the Church of England* (London 1618) 91

22 Peter Smart, *The Vanitie and Downe-fall of Superstitious Popish Ceremonies* (Edinburgh 1628) 6

23 In his *Defence of the Innocencie* Cestren outlines these 'Opinions,' as he calls them, in an 'Epistle to the Non-conformists.'

24 John Gauden, *Considerations Touching the Liturgy of the Church of England* (London 1661) 9–10

25 Ibid, 10

26 The original of the *Notes* of Andrewes has never been found, but there are two transcriptions, one done by Cosin in 1619. The Cosin transcription can be found in the *Works* of Andrewes in the volume with 'Two Answers ... Perron,' 145–57

27 Amy Charles has interesting information about Thomas Laurence, Herbert's successor at Bemerton, in 'Appendix E' of her *Life* of George Herbert: in 1646 Laurence was charged with introducing innovations in the Church. But, as should be clear by now, I am not as sure as she that this evidence suggests nothing of what might have been Herbert's own practices during his tenure.

28 'A Preparation to Prayer,' in *Ninety-Six Sermons*, vol 5, 349

29 Ibid, 407

30 Izaak Walton, *The Lives* intro George Saintsbury (London: Oxford University Press) 289

31 Lancelot Andrewes, *Institutiones Paie: or, Directions to Pray* (London 1633) 112

32 Herbert Thorndike, *Of the Laws of the Church* (1659) in *Works*, vol 4 (1852) 729–30

33 Andrewes, *Institutiones Piae*, 110–11

34 John Prideaux, *Euchologia: or, the Doctrine of Practical Praying* (London 1655) 59–60

35 Herbert's mention of his copy of the *Works* of St Augustine in his Will, of course, assures almost everyone that Augustine was important to him. It is what to do with the fact, how to interpret it, that is the problem.

36 See my article 'David's Successors: Forms of Joy and Art,' *Proceedings of the Patristic, Medieval, and Renaissance Conference* 2 (1977) 31–7. The *verbum vocis-verbum cordis* distinction can be found throughout Augustine, but especially important for this is the *Commentary on John*.

37 Donne, *Sermons*, vol 3, 368

38 The Prayer-Book has it (p 708).

39 Henry Hammond, *A Vindication of the Ancient Liturgie of the Church of England* (London 1660) 17

40 John Gauden, *Considerations*, 1–2

41 Andrewes, *A Preparation to Prayer*, 349

42 There are several passages in *The Country Parson* which I could have quoted to make the point opposite from the one I am making, and I suggest that one of the interpretive difficulties we have here is created by the middleness of the way. But also we do the man a serious wrong if we do not allow him to change his mind. Was he the same man at Bemerton that he was at Cambridge? Was it not, perhaps, for a very good reason that Herbert left out his original version of 'The H. Communion' entirely from *The Temple* and replaced it with a far more thoughtful poem?

43 Augustine, *Psalms Commentary*, vol 2, 233–4

44 Augustine, *On the Gospel of John* trans James Innes, in *Works*, vol 11 (Edinburgh 1874) 509 (tract 118)

45 William Laud, *A Sermon Preached on Monday, the Seauenteenth of March, at Westminster: At the Opening of Parliament* (London 1628) 4, 9.

46 Richard Baxter, *Catholic Communion* (London 1684) 13. This use of 'analogically' here and the response to it provokes him to add in another tract later that all analogy is equivocation.

47 Ibid, 18

48 Andrewes, *Notes*, 156–7

49 *An Augustine Reader* ed John O'Meara (New York: Doubleday 1973) 197

50 See Barbara Leah Harman's interesting article in *PMLA* 93 (1978) 865–77: 'The Fiction of Coherence: George Herbert's "The Collar."' Certainly much more should be done with the reflexiveness of Herbert's poetry too. It talks about itself and reacts to itself.

51 *An Augustine Reader*, 200–1

52 Thomas Cestren, *Defence of the Innocencie*, 54

CHAPTER FOUR

1 See here the important article by James Thorpe, 'Reflections and Self-Reflections.' Also see Rosemond Tuve, 'George Herbert and *Caritas*.'

2 Augustine, *Psalms Commentary*, vol 1, 308–9 (Psalm 33)

3 Francis Taylor, *An Exposition with Practicall Observations upon the three first Chapters of the Proverbs* (London 1655) 7

4 Taylor, *An Exposition ... upon the three first*, 11

5 Michael Jermin, *Paraphrastical Meditations*, 30

6 The notion of the 'garment of style' is, of course, at work here. Wisdom as trim dress and, particularly, the trim dress of the Mother-Church, is looked at further in the next chapter.

7 Jermin, *Paraphrastical Meditations*, 478

8 John Dod and Robert Cleaver, *A Plaine and Familiar Exposition of the Thirteenth and Fourteenth Chapter of the Proverbs of Salomon* (London 1615) 7–8

9 Robert Cleaver, *A Plaine and Familiar Exposition of the First and Second Chapters of the Proverbs of Salomon* (London 1614) 20

10 Taylor, *An Exposition ... upon the three first*, 7

11 Origen, *The Song of Songs: Commentary and Homilies* trans R.P. Lawson (London 1957) 41

12 Jermin, *Paraphrastical Meditations*, 5

13 Ibid, 353, 199

14 Cleaver, *A Plaine and Familiar*, 22

15 The 'old age' of the Church is discussed similarly by John Dod and Robert Cleaver in *A Plaine and Familiar Exposition of the Fifteenth, Sixteenth and Seventeenth Chapters of the Proverbs of Salomon* (London 1611), 104: 'The head is deckt with *gray haires*, and the heart with heavenly graces, and the *life with virtuous behaviour*, he is more gorgeously apparelled then if otherwise he were clad in gold ... What though their strength be diminished, and their memories impaired? *What though they retaine not their former freshnesse of wit, or elegancie of speech?*'

16 As in Latin and in Greek, no copula is needed to predicate: *Beatus vir*, blessed is the man.

17 My own image of George Herbert is of a man who thought about the structure and meaning of almost everything, including faith. The thoughtless acceptance implied by the first Communion poem, excluded from *The Temple*, is, I think, quite uncharacteristic and, with good reason I suspect, he changed it.

18 Taylor, *An Exposition ... upon the three first*, 2

19 Origen, *The Song of Songs*, 43–4

20 Here Herbert separates himself in a major way from Francis Bacon, whose influence on Herbert still needs further investigation.

21 Taylor, *An Exposition ... upon the three first*, 12

22 William Pemble, *Salomons Recantation and Repentance* (London 1627), 'Epistle Dedicatory.'

23 Donne, *Sermons*, vol 3, 47

24 Cleaver, *A Plaine and Familiar*, 120–1

25 Thomas Granger, *A Familiar Exposition or Commentarie on Ecclesiastes* (London 1601) 309

26 Granger, *A Familiar Exposition*, 114–15

27 William Perkins, 'The Art of Prophecying,' intro Thomas Tuke in *The Workes*, vol 2

28 Michael Jermin, *A Commentarie upon the Whole Booke of Ecclesiastes* (London 1639) 446

29 Sidney's distinction between philosophy and history as the difference between precept and example, with poetry combining the best of both, imperfectly, is of some importance here. Herbert understands the precept to be in the example, in Christian tradition; but the distinction fascinates him, as in 'Lent.'

30 See Hutchinson's note on this poem and the Character.

31 Origen, *The Song of Songs*, 53

32 Henry Lok, *Ecclesiastes, otherwise called the Preacher* (London 1597), 'To the Christian Reader'

33 William Gouge, *An Exposition of the Song of Solomon* (London 1615), 'To the Christian Reader'

34 Origen, *The Song of Songs*, 24

35 George Gyffard, *Fifteene Sermons upon the Song of Solomon* (London 1598), 'Epistle Dedicatory'

36 William Guild, *Loves Entercours between The Lamb & his Bride* (London 1657) 5

37 Jos. Hall, *An Open and Plaine Paraphrase, upon the Song of Songs* (London 1609), 'Epistle Dedicatory'

38 Robert Bellarmine, *The Ascent of the Mind to God by a Ladder of Things Created* intro James Brodrick (London 1928) xv

39 John Dove, *The Conversion of Solomon* (London 1613) 169

40 St Bernard, *Cantica Canticorum: Eighty-six Sermons on the Song of Solomon* trans Samuel J. Eales (London 1895) 113

41 John Dove, *The Conversion*, 17–18, 102

42 John Cotton, *A Brief Exposition of the whole Book of Canticles, or Song of Solomon* (London 1642) 9

43 This sounds like an emblem, and there may very well be a source for this that Herbert shares with Crashaw.

44 Bernard, *Cantica Canticorum*, 508

45 Augustine, *Psalms Commentary*, vol 1, 240 (Psalm 31)

46 See, for instance, Donne *Sermons*, vol 5, 270–1; and vol 6, 39; 'upon no premises doth any conclusion follow, so logically, so sincerely, so powerfully, so imperiously, so undeniably, as upon this, *the Lord hath, and therefore the Lord will.*'

47 See, for one, John Day, *Day's Descant on David's Psalmes: or A Commentary upon the Psalter, as it is usually read throughout the yeare at Morning and Evening Prayer* (Oxford 1620) 116

48 This is at the conclusion of 'The Printers to the Reader,' reprinted in the Hutchinson edition. Donne has a sermon on this text (*Sermons*, vol 1).

49 Augustine, *Psalms Commentary*, vol 1, 160 (Psalm 22)

50 Augustine, *Psalms Commentary*, vol 6, 240 (Psalm 141)

CHAPTER FIVE

1 *Sermons*, vol 8, 90

2 *Latin Poetry*, 'Corneliae sanctae,' 129

3 Ibid, 125

4 Ibid, 127

5 *Latin Poetry*, 'Μῆτερ, γυναικῶν αἴγλη,' 149

6 See Cicero, *Topica* trans H.M. Hubbell (Cambridge, Mass.: Loeb 1949) 409. Also *The Logicke of the Moste Excellent Philosopher P. Ramus Martyr* trans Roland MacIlmaine (1574), ed Catherine M. Dunn (San Fernando Valley State College, California: Renaissance Editions 1969) 29–33.

7 Walton, *The Lives*, 266

8 Donne, *Sermons*, vol 9, 192–3

9 Lancelot Andrewes, *Sermons* ed G.M. Story (Oxford: Clarendon 1967) 194

10 *Sermons*, vol 9, 201

11 *Sermons*, vol 5, 368

12 *Sermons*, vol 9, 209

13 Walton, *The Lives*, 308

14 Helen Meredith Garth, *Saint Mary Magdalene in Medieval Literature* (Johns Hopkins University Studies in Historical and Political Science, series 67, 1950) 78

15 Ibid, 78

16 Ibid, 98

17 Johannes Smeaton, *S. Mary Magdalens Pilgrimage to Paradise* (London 1617) 137–8

18 *Latin Poetry*, 'Aἰάζω γενέτειραν,' 153

19 Quoted from *The Divine Poetry of John Donne* ed Helen Gardner (Oxford: Clarendon Press 1952)

20 *Sermons*, vol 1, 285

21 *Sermons*, vol 8, 237

22 *Sermons*, vol 9, 193

23 *Sermons*, vol 9, 76–7

24 *Sermons*, vol 6, 284

25 See Ronald Wardhaugh, *Introduction to Linguistics* (New York: McGraw-Hill 1972) 161; and the work of Michael Gregory.

26 Henry Peacham, *The Garden of Eloquence*, a facsimile reproduction, intro William G. Crane (Gainesville, Fla. 1954) 21

27 Clearly, *latus*, the fourth principle part of *fero*, is at the core of the hermeneutic here.

28 *The Country Parson*, 282

29 Robert Southwell, *Mary Magdalens Funerall Teares* (London 1602)

30 G. Markham, *Marie Magdalens Lamentations for the Losse of her Master Jesus* (London 1601)

31 Southwell, 4

32 Ibid, 6

33 Ibid, 68

34 G. Markham, *Marie Magdalens Lamentations*

35 Wilcoks, *Six Sermons*, 45
36 Southwell, 52
37 *Sermons*, 210
38 *Sermons*, vol 9, 76–7
39 *Sermons*, vol 9, 210
40 *Sermons*, vol 9, 211
41 *Sermons*, vol 9, 75–6
42 *Sermons*, vol 1, 199
43 Andrewes, *Sermons*, 208
44 *Latin Poetry*, 'Quid nugor calamo,' 131
45 *Latin Poetry*, 'Pallida materni Genii,' 139
46 *Sermons*, 210
47 *Latin Poetry*, 'Quid nugor calamo,' 131
48 Cestren, *Defence*, 291
49 Wilcoks, *Six Sermons*, 45
50 Ibid, 54
51 Ibid, 58
52 Ibid, 61
53 Andrewes, *Ninety-Six Sermons*, vol 4, 40
54 Lancelot Andrewes, *Stricturae: or, A Briefe Answer to the XVIII Chapter of the first Booke of Cardinall Perron's Reply* (London 1629) 1
55 *Sermons*, vol 9, 203
56 *Latin Poetry*, 'Ψυχης ασθενὲς,' 149
57 *Sermons*, vol 9, 79
58 *Sermons*, vol 1, 282–3
59 *Sermons*, vol 7, 280–1
60 *Sermons*, vol 7, 297

A Bibliography of
Exegetical and Doctrinal Materials

Ainsworth, Henry *Annotations Upon the Five Bookes of Moses, the Booke of The Psalmes, and the Song of Songs, Canticles* London 1627

Allen, Robert *An Alphabet of the Holy Proverbs of King Solomon* London 1596

Andrewes, Lancelot *Institutiones Piae: or, Directions to Pray* London 1633

– *Ninety-Six Sermons* Oxford 1843

– *Notes on the Book of Common Prayer*

– *A Pattern of Catechistical Doctrine* 1630; rpt Oxford

– *Stricture: or, A Briefe Answer to the* XVIII *Chapter of the first Booke of Cardinall Perron's Reply* London 1629

– *Two Answers to Cardinal Perron* Oxford 1854

Aquinas: A Collection of Critical Essays ed Anthony Kenny, London 1969

An Aquinas Reader ed Mary T. Clark, New York 1972

Aristotle *The Categories* trans Harold P. Cook, Cambridge, Mass. 1938

Augustine *City of God* in *Works* vol 1, Edinburgh 1871

– *Confessions* trans I.G. Pilkington, in *Works* vol 14, Edinburgh 1876

– *Expositions on the Book of Psalms* A Library of Fathers, 6 vols, Oxford 1847

– *On Christian Doctrine* trans D.W. Robertson, Jr, New York 1958

– *On Music* trans Robert Catesby Taliaferro, in *The Fathers of the Church* New York 1947

– *On the Catechising of the Uninstructed* trans S.D. Salmond, in *Works* vol 9, Edinburgh 1873

– *On the Gospel of John* trans James Innes, in *Works* vol 10–11, Edinburgh 1874

– *On the Spirit and the Letter* London 1925

– *Soliloquies* trans Thomas F. Gilligan, O.S.A., in *The Fathers of the Church* New York 1948

– *The Trinity* trans Stephen McKenna, Washington 1963

Austin, William *Devotionis Augustinianae Flamma* London 1635

Baldwin, William *A Treatise of Moral Philosophe* 1547: facs, rpt with intro by Robert Hood Bowers, Gainsville, Fla. 1967

Bancroft, Richard *A Sermon Preached at Paules Cross the 9 of Februarie 1588* London 1588 [1 John 4:1]

Barr, James *The Semantics of Biblical Language* Oxford 1961

I.B. [John Bate] *The Psalme of Mercy: or, A Meditation upon the 51 Ps* London 1625

Baxter, Richard *An Account of the Reasons ... Communion* London 1684

- *Catholic Communion* London 1684

- *Catholic Communion Doubly Defended: By Dr. Owen's Vindicator and Richard Baxter* London 1684

- *Certain Disputations of Right to Sacraments and the True Nature of Visible Christianity* London 1658

- *Poetical Fragments: Heart-Imployment with God and Itself* London 1681

Bellarmine, Robert *The Ascent of the Mind to God by a Ladder of Things Created* trans T.B. for 1st ed 1616; rpt with intro by James Brodrick, London 1928

Bernard *Cantica Canticorum: Eighty-six Sermons of the Song of Solomon* trans Samuel J. Eales, London 1895

- *Life and Works of Saint Bernard* ed John Mabillon, 4 vols, London 1895

- *On the Love of God* trans Edmund G. Gardner, London 1915

R.B. [Richard Bernard] and R.A. *David's Musick or Psalmes ... Unfolded Logically* London 1616

Beza, Theodore *Christian Meditations upon eight Psalms of the Prophet David* trans J.S.A., London 1582

- *Ecclesiastes, or the Preacher* Cambridge 1593

Bird, Samuel *The Lectures of Samuel Bird ... upon the Eighth and Ninth Chapters of the Second Epistle to the Corinthians* Cambridge 1598

- *The Lectures of Samuel Bird ... and upon the 38 Psalme* Cambridge 1598

Bonaventure *Itinerarium Mentis en Deum, The Franciscan Vision* trans Father James, London 1937

- *The Mirror of the Blessed Virgin Mary* trans L.G., Dublin 1849

- *The Mystical Vine: A Treatise on the Passion of Our Lord* London 1955

- *The Six Wings of the Seraphim* trans Dominic Devas, in *A Franciscan View* London 1922

Boys, John *An Exposition of Al the Principall Scriptures Used in our English Liturgie* London 1610

- *An Exposition of the Last Psalme* London 1613

Bradshaw, William *A Meditation of Man's Mortalitie Containing an Exposition of the Ninetieth Psalme* London 1621

Bridges, William *Jacob's Counsell and King David's Seasonable Hearing It* London 1642

Brook, Stella *The Language of the Book of Common Prayer* London 1965

Broughton, Hugh *A Comment upon Coheleth of Ecclesiastes* London 1605

Bulwer, John *Chirologia: or the Naturall Language of the Hand.* London, 1644

Buggs, Samuel *Davids Strait* London 1622 [2 Samuel 24:14]

Burke, Kenneth *The Rhetoric of Religion: Studies in Logology* Berkeley and Los Angeles 1970

Burton, William *Davids Evidence or the Assurance of Gods Love* 1592 [Psalm 41:11–13]

– *David's Thankes-giving* London 1602 [Psalm 10:17–18]

Byfield, N. *An Exposition upon the Epistle to the Colossians* London 1617

Calvin, John *A Commentarie of M. John Caluine upon the Epistle to the Colossians* trans R.V., London 1581

– *A Commentarie upon S. Paules Epistles to the Corinthians* trans Thomas Tymme, London 1577

– *Commentary on the Book of Psalms* trans from the original Latin and collated with the author's French version, 5 vols, Edinburgh 1845

Caryl, Joseph *David's Prayer for Solomon* Oxford, 1643

Cassiodorus *An Introduction to Divine and Human Readings* trans Leslie Webber Jones, New York 1946

Cave, Terence C. *Devotional Poetry in France, 1570–1613* Cambridge 1969

Cestren, Thomas *Defence of the Innocencie of the Three Ceremonies of the Church of England* London 1618

Chomsky, William *Hebrew: The Eternal Language* Philadelphia 1957

Chrysostom *The Homilies of S. John Chrysostom on the First Epistle of St. Paul the Apostle to the Corinthians* Oxford 1839

– *The Homilies of S. John Chrysostom ... on the Second Epistle of St. Paul ... to the Corinthians* Oxford 1848

– *Of Praying unto God in Certain Treatises of the Ancient Holy Fathers, Touching the Doctrine of Good Woorkes* London 1569

– *Of the Priesthood* trans Henry Hollier, London 1728

Cleaver, Robert *A Plaine and Familiar Exposition of the First and Second Chapters of the Proverbs of Solomon* London 1614

Colish, Marcia L. *The Mirror of Language* New Haven 1968

Concise Oxford Dictionary of the Christian Church ed E.A. Livingstone, Oxford 1977

Conway, Moncure Daniel *Solomon and Solomonic Literature* New York 1973

Cosin, John *The Correspondence of John Cosin* London 1869

– *The History of Transubstantiation* London 1676

– 'Notes on the Book of Common Prayer' in *Works* vol 5, Oxford 1855

Cotton, John *A Brief Exposition of the whole Book of Canticles, or Song of Solomon* London 1642

Coverdale, Miles *Remains of Myles Coverdale* ed George Pearson, Cambridge 1846
– *Writings and Translations of Myles Coverdale* ed George Pearson, Cambridge 1844
Cowper, William *A Holy Alphabet for Sion's Scholars ... Delivered, by way of Commentary, upon the whole 119 Psalme* London 1613
– *The Triumph of a Christian* London 1639
Daniélou, Jean *Origen* trans Walter Mitchell, New York 1955
Davies, Horton *Worship and Theology in England: From Andrewes to Baxter and Fox* Princeton 1975
Day, John *David's Desire to Goe to Church* Oxford 1615
– *Day's Descant on David's Psalmes: or A Commentary upon the Psalter, as it is usually read throughout the yeare at Morning and Evening Prayer* Oxford 1620
Dickson, David *An Exposition of All St. Pauls Epistles* London 1659
Dod, John, and Cleaver, Robert *A Plaine and Familiar Exposition: of the Eighteenth Nineteenth, and Twentieth Chapters of the Proverbs of Solomon* London 1611
– *A Plaine and Familiar Exposition of the Eleventh and Twelfth Chapters of the Proverbs of Solomon* London 1612
– *A Plaine and Familiar Exposition of the Fifteenth Sixteenth, and Seventeenth Chapters of the Proverbs of Solomon* London 1611
– *A Plaine and Familiar Exposition of the Ninth and Tenth Chapters of the Proverbs of Solomon* London 1612
– *A Plaine and Familiar Exposition of the Thirteenth and Fourteenth Chapters of the Proverbs of Solomon* London 1615
– *A Profitable Metaphrase upon the Epistle of Paul to the Colossians* London 1609
Dod, John, and Hinde, William *Bathshebae's Instructions to her Sonne, Lemuel* London 1614
Donne, John *The Sermons of John Donne* ed Evelyn M. Simpson and George R. Potter, 10 vols, Berkeley and Los Angeles 1953–62
Dove, John *The Conversion of Solomon* London 1613
Drijvers, Pius *The Psalms: Their Structure and Meaning* New York 1964
Emminghaus, Johannes H. *Mary Magdalene* London 1967
Erasmus, Desiderius *The Colloquies of Erasmus* trans Craig R. Thompson, Chicago 1965
Farrar, Austin *Reflective Faith* ed Charles C. Conti. Grand Rapids, Michigan 1974
Ferguson, James *A Brief Exposition of the Epistles of Paul to the Galatians and Ephesians* London 1659
Ferrar, Nicholas *The Story Books of Little Gidding* intro E. Cruwys Sharland, New York 1899
The Ferrar Papers ed B. Blackstone, Cambridge 1938
Five Pastorals: Works on the Ministry by William Perkins, George Herbert, Thomas Fuller and Richard Baxter ed Thomas Woods, London 1961

Fletcher, Phineas *The Way to Blessednes, A Treatise or Commentary, on the First Psalme* London 1632

Garth, Helen Meredith *Saint Mary Magdalen in Mediaeval Literature* Johns Hopkins University's Studies in Historical and Political Science, ser 67, 1950

Gataker, Thomas *David's Instructer: A Sermon* London 1620 [Psalm 34:11]

– *David's Remembrancer: A Meditation on Psalme 13.1* London 1623

– *Gods Parley with Princes* London 1620 [Psalm 82]

– *Jacob's Thankfulnesse to God ... A Meditation on Gen. 32:10* London 1624

Gauden, John *Considerations Touching the Liturgy of the Church of England* London 1661 [Ephesians 6:18]

Gordis, Robert *Koheleth – The Man and His World* New York 1951

Gouge, William *An Exposition of the Song of Solomon* London 1615

– *The Saints Sacrifice: Or, A Commentarie on the cxvi Psalme* London 1632

Granger, Thomas *A Familiar Exposition or Commentarie on Ecclesiastes* London 1621

Gregory the Great *Dialogues* trans Odo John Zimmerman, O.S.B., in *The Fathers of the Church* New York 1959

– *Pastoral Care* trans Henry Davis, Westminster, Maryland 1950

Guild, William *Loves Entercours between The Lamb & His Bride* London 1657

Gyffard, George *Fifteene Sermons upon the Song of Solomon* London 1598

Hakewill, George *King Davids Vow for Reformation of Himselfe* London 1621 [Psalm 101]

Hall, Joseph *An Open and Plaine Paraphrase upon the Song of Songs* London 1609

Hammond, Henry *A Vindication of the Ancient Liturgie of the Church of England* London 1660

Hayward, John *David's teares* London 1632

Herbert, George *The Latin Poetry of George Herbert* trans Mark McCloskey and Paul R. Murphy, Athens, Ohio 1965

– *The Works of George Herbert* ed F.E. Hutchinson, Oxford 1941

Herle, Charles *Wisedomes Tripos* London 1655

Hieron, Sam. *Davids Penitentiall Psalme Opened* Cambridge 1615 [Psalm 51]

Hirsch, E.D., Jr *Validity in Interpretation* New Haven 1967

Hodson, Phineas *The Kings Request: Or, David's Desire* London 1628 [Psalm 27:4]

Holland, Henry *Davids Faith and Repentance* London 1589 [Psalm 32:5]

Hooper, John *Certain Comfortable Expositions of the Constant Martyr of Christ* London 1580 [Psalms 23, 61, 73, 77]

Horn, Robert *The Shield of the Righteous: Or, The Ninety First Psalme, Expounded* London 1625

Hugh of St Victor *Didascalicon* trans Jerome Taylor, New York 1961

– *On the Sacraments of the Christian Faith* trans Roy J. Deferrari, Cambridge, Mass, 1951

– *Soliloquy on the Earnest Money of the Soul* trans Kevin Herbert, Milwaukee 1956
Hutchens, E. *Davids Sling against Great Goliath* London 1593
Hutton, Thomas *Reasons for the Refusal of Subscription to the booke of Common Prayer ... With an Answere* London 1605
Iranaeus *The Writings of Iranaeus* trans Alexander Roberts and W.H. Rambaut, Edinburgh 1868
Jackson, Thomas *Davids Pastorall Poem: or Sheepheards Song* London 1603
Jermin, Michael *A Commentarie upon the Whole Book of Ecclesiastes* London 1639
– *Paraphrastical Meditations ... Commentarie upon the Whole Booke of the Proverbs of Solomon* London 1638
Jerome *The Homilies of Saint Jerome* trans Sister Marie Liguori Ewald, J.H.M., in *The Fathers of the Church* 2 vols, Washington 1964
Jewell, John *The Works* London 1609
Johnson, Robert *Davids Teacher* London 1609 [Psalm 119:33]
King, Henry *David's Enlargement* Oxford 1625 [Psalm 32:5]
– *David's Strait* Oxford 1625 [2 Samuel 24:14]
Laud, William *A Speech Delivered in the Starr Chamber* London 1637
Leigh, Edward *Critica Sacra: or Philological and Theological Observations* London 1639
Leigh, William *Davids Palme and Cedar* London 1614 [Psalm 92:12–15]
Lewis, C.S. *Reflections on the Psalms* New York 1958
Lok, Henry *Ecclesiastes, otherwise called the Preacher* London 1597
Lucy, William *A Treatise of the Nature of a Minister* London 1670
Luther, Martin *An Exposition of Solomon's Booke called Ecclesiastes or the Preacher* trans John Day, London 1573
– *A Very Excellent and Swete Exposition upon the xxii Psalme* trans Myles Coverdale, 1538 [Psalm 23]
Macquarrie, John *Principles of Christian Theology* New York 1966
Meyer, John *The English Catechisme* London 1621
Milwarde, John *Jacob's Great Day of Trouble and Deliverance* London 1610
Montagu, Richard *Appello Caesarem* London 1625
– *Immediate Addresse unto God Alone* London 1624
More, Paul Elmer, and Cross, Frank Leslie *Anglicanism* London 1962
Morton, Thomas *The Encounter Against M. Parsons* London 1610
Moran, Gabriel *Theology of Revelation* New York 1966
Nicholson, William *A Plaine but Full Exposition of the Catechism of the Church of England* London 1662
Ong, Walter J., S.J. *Ramus, Method, and the Decay of Dialogue* Cambridge., Mass. 1958

Origen *The Song of Songs: Commentary and Homilies* trans R.P. Lawson, London 1957

Osiander, Andrew *A Sermon out of the xci Psalme* trans Myles Coverdale, 1538

Overton, John *Jacob's Troublesome Journey to Bethel* Oxford 1586

Peacham, Henry *The Garden of Eloquence* 1593; fasc rpt with intro by William G. Crane, Gainseville, Fla. 1954

Pemble, William *Salomon's Recantation and Repentance* London 1627

Perkins, William 'The Art of Prophecying' in *The Workes* vol 2, trans Thomas Tuke, London 1635

– 'A Direction for the Government of the Tongue according to God's Word' in *The Workes* vol 1, London 1635

– *A Godly and Learned Exposition or Commentarie upon The Three First Chapters of the Revelation* London 1631

Prideaux, John *David's Rejoycing for Christ's Resurrection* Oxford 1636 [Psalm 16:10, 11]

– *Euchologia* 1655

Puttenham, George *The Arte of English Poesie* ed Gladys Willcock and Alice Walker, Cambridge 1936

Quarles, Francis *Solomon's Recantation* London 1645

Ramsey, Ian T. *Religious Language* London 1957

Reading, John *Davids Soliloquie* London 1627 [Psalm 42:11]

Reynolds, Edward *An Explication of the Hundreth and Tenth Psalme* London 1632

Ridley, Lancelot *An Exposicion in Englishe upon the Epistle of S. Paule, to the Colossians* London 1548

Ringgren, Helmer *Word and Wisdom* Lund 1947

Roberts, Alexander *An Exposition upon the Hundred and Thirtie Psalme* London 1610

Rogers, Daniel *David's Cost* London 1619 [2 Samuel 24:24]

Rollok, Robert *An Exposition upon some Select Psalme of David* Edinburgh 1600

Saunders, Nicholas *The Supper of Our Lord* London 1566

Schmaus, Michael *The Church as Sacrament* in *Dogma* vol 5, Kansas City 1975

Serranus, John *A Godlie and Learned Commentarie Upon … Ecclesiastes* trans John Stockwood, London 1585

Smart, Peter *The Vanitie and Downe-fall of Superstitious Popish Ceremonies* Edinburgh 1628

Smecton, Johannes *S. Mary Magdalen's Pilgrimage to Paradise* London 1617

Smith, Samuel *The Chiefe Shepheard: or, An Exposition upon ye xxiii Psalme* London 1625

– *Davids Blessed Man* London 1617 [Psalm 1]

– *Davids Repentence* London 1616 [Psalm 51]

Starkey, Thomas *An Exhortation to the People* London 1540

Stonham, Mathew *A Treatise on the First Psalme* London 1610

Strigelius, Victorinus *Part of the Harmony of King David's Harp* trans Richard Robinson, London 1582

– *A Proceeding in the Harmonie of King David's Harpe* trans Robinson, London 1591

– *A Third Proceeding in the Harmonie of King David's Harp* trans Richard Robinson, London 1595

Symson, A. *A Sacred Septenarie; or A Godly Exposition on the Seven Psalms of Repentence* London 1623

Tavard, George *The Quest for Catholicity* New York: Herder & Herder 1964

Taylor, Francis *An Exposition With Practicall Observations upon the 4, 5, 6, 7, 8, 9 Chapters of the Proverbs* London 1657

– *An Exposition with Practicall Observations upon the Three First Chapters of the Proverbs* London 1655

Taylor, Thomas *A Commentarie upon the Epistle of S. Paul written to Titus* London 1612

– *Davids Learning, or the Way to True Happinesse: In a Commentarie upon the xxxii Psalme* London 1618

Temple, W. *A Logical Analysis of Twenty Select Psalmes* London 1605

Thomas à Kempis *Imitation of Christ* ed Harold C. Gardiner, s.j., New York 1955

Thorndike, Herbert *Theological Works* Oxford 1844

Turnbull, Richard *An Exposition upon the xv Psalme* London 1592

Ussher, James *An Answer to a Challenge Made by a Jesuite* London 1631 [Matthew 19:8]

– *A Body of Divinitie, or the Summe and Substance of Christian Religion* London 1645

– *The Substance of that which was delivered in a Sermon Before the Commons House of Parliament in St. Margarets Church at Westminister, the 18 of February, 1620* London 1621

Vertue, Henry *Christ and the Church, or Parallels* London 1659

Von Rad, Gerhard *Wisdom in Israel* London 1972

Webbe, William *A Discourse of English Poetrie* English Reprints, London 1870

Whitby, Daniel *A Paraphrase and Commentary upon all the Epistles of the New Testament* London 1700

Wilcoks, John *Six Sermons* London 1641

Wilcox, Thomas *An Exposition uppon the Booke of Canticles* London 1585

Willet, Andrew *Ecclesia Triumphans ... With a briefe Exposition of the 122 Psalme* Cambridge 1614

Wilson, Thomas *The Arte of Rhetorique* 1553; facs rpt with intro by Robert Hood Bowers, Gainsville, Fla. 1962

– *The Rule of Reason conteinying the Arte of Logike* London 1563
Wither, George *A Preparation to the Psalter* Manchester 1884
– *Psalms of David* Manchester 1881
Wright, John *The Deliverance of the Whole House of Israel* London 1641 [Romans 2]

Index